MADE FREE

Embrace a Life Lived in Freedom

By

Tracy L. Edwards

© 2020 by Tracy L. Edwards

Publisher information

Library of Congress Cataloging-in-Publication Data

Edwards, Tracy L., 1966–
        MADE FREE / Embrace a Life Lived in Freedom

ISBN 978-1-7355944-0-8 (softcover)

CONTENTS

DEDICATION

To the One who made me free, Almighty God.
To my husband, Steve: I love you.
To my children and grandchildren: always chose to live in true freedom.

INTRODUCTION

This book wasn't written to be a quick and easy read. It is my hope that as you read through it, you'll take the necessary time to process the principles so you can continually be made free by the goodness of God.

You are so courageous to begin this journey, even if you have doubts and maybe a little bit of fear. God loves you, and He is with you through every step. His passion is to see you to fulfill the thoughts He has for you, thoughts of peace, to give you a hope and a future.

You will struggle with some of the things written in this book. Trust the Holy Spirit to lead you through.

You will have to face some difficult things, about yourself and others. Trust that Jesus Christ will never leave nor forsake you.

You may want to give up. Trust that if God is for you, who can be against you?

Your life is the greatest gift to God and to the people around you.

Be made free so that you can live free all the days of your life.

Enjoy the greatest journey ever. Yours!

In Him I Live,
Tracy L. Edwards
Up-Word@outlook.com

"Heavenly Father, through Your love we are made free. You are the Author and Finisher of our faith. So, by the power of Your Holy Spirit, help us to choose and live in the freedom found only through a personal relationship with Jesus Christ. I pray You will continually reveal to us that true freedom is found in your loving commands. I pray that as we are transformed by Your Truths, we become more like Jesus Christ every day. May our journey give You glory.

In Jesus' Name I pray. Amen."

PART ONE

Laying the Foundation

Foundations are important. Jesus teaches about the consequences of building your life upon a solid foundation as opposed to upon shifting sand.

> *"Therefore whoever hears these sayings of Mine, and does them, I will liken him to a wise man who built his house on the rock: and the rain descended, the floods came, and the winds blew and beat on that house; and it did not fall, for it was founded on the rock.*
>
> *"But everyone who hears these sayings of Mine, and does not do them, will be like a foolish man who built his house on the sand: and the rain descended, the floods came, and the winds blew and beat on that house; and it fell. And great was its fall."* (Matthew 7:24-27)

Our lives were meant to be built on the solid foundation of the principles of God. Every other foundation will not stand.

Because many of us have foundations which are not solid and based on Truth, God takes us through a process to tear down anything that is not of Him and damaging to us. Then He builds us up on the Rock, so that when life events happen, we are not destroyed.

Please do not be deceived that you will only have to go through

1

foundational, complete repairs or maintenance once. It's a lifelong process, but it does get easier each round. God's restoration process usually goes in layers. One layer of hurt, incorrect belief, and correction at a time. It is, I believe, a protective measure for us. But there will be times when He uses the same situation, or type of situation, to reveal something more.

His process of growth to get us to maturity in our freedom in Christ sometimes is mistaken for "We didn't get it right the first time." It's not about getting it right; it is about continual healing, restoration, and then being entrusted with greater things, for His glory and our good.

As we experience more and more freedom in Christ, when He takes us back to our past—to learn, not live there again—we can see things from a healthier, healed perspective. No longer distorted through the lens of youth, lack of understanding, pain, and/or self-preservation.

Foundation checks are important. Wear and tear happens because life happens. So, incorporate foundation checks in your life-long journey with the Lord.

CHAPTER 1

The Heart of the Father

"He who does not love does not know God, for God is love."
(1 John 4:8)

Perspective. According to the 1828 Noah Webster's Dictionary, which I love, perspective is defined as '*a glass through which objects are viewed*'. Each of us processes every life experience—mentally, physically, emotionally, and spiritually—through our individual-looking glass; our personal perspective. Every experience or new piece of information will either bring clarity or distortion to our perspective and how we process life and the world around us.

Why is perspective so important? Because the way we see God defines how we see ourselves, those around us, life circumstances, world events, and everything else in the universe. Our perspective of God is the foundation upon which everything else is built.

If your perspective is that there is no God, then every thought, decision, and life encounter is filtered through the attitude that you are your own moral compass. Individual moral compasses may believe that there is no life after death; the earth is just on a timer; and/or a person can do whatever they want without any higher-power consequences.

If your perspective is that God is angry, vengeful or distant, then thoughts, actions, relationships, and perception of self are seen, defined, and responded to based on those same perspectives.

If your perspective of God is based on an earthly father or father-figure, then the ensuing view of all else in life can swing the full breadth of a pendulum. The best of fathers, those who provide a safe home and loving care, are still imperfect and do not embody the fullness of who God is and His role as Father. Those whose father, or father-figures, were absent or operated in abuse or violence, have a distorted perspective of who God is in unimaginable ways. If your father operated with any degree of abuse, I am so, so sorry you were exposed to, or experienced any degree of, mistreatment. I know for many of you it may be difficult to hear this right now, but it is not Father God's heart, nor Will, for you to have encountered abuse of any kind. It is His heart to bring healing and to restore you to the fullness of whom He formed you to be (Jeremiah 29:11).

If your perspective is that God is good and He loves you, you're not off the hook. I'm going to challenge you to come to a higher perspective and embrace a deeper revelation of Almighty God as our Father, God (Romans 8:15).

Before we get to the heart of the Father, allow me to attempt to describe who God is. It's important for you to either begin to understand the magnitude of God or enlarge your understanding of who He is. Seeing life filtered through the perspective of who God is defines how you view everything—from a seed, to the vastness of space and time. Most importantly, knowing God in all His attributes defines how you perceive yourself and others.
Knowing Him as Creator, for example, lays the foundation to view our self and others with intrinsic value simply because we were created by the Creator, in His image (Genesis 1:26). Viewing life through the perspective that we somehow evolved from 'whatever' establishes a train of thought which quickly diminishes our innate value that we, as human beings, possess.

Living life from the perspective that God gives hope, which He does, allows you to process mistakes, tragedy, and pain with the optimism that mistakes can be overcome, tragedy can be survived, and pain will be healed. If you live life with the perspective that God leaves you on your own through life, then hope, if it exists, is rooted in self or others, and is therefore fleeting. The hope God provides is rooted in eternity and is definitely not fleeting (Ecclesiastes 3:11).

Are you beginning to see why your perspective of God is so important? It is the foundation that defines everything about you and life. This chapter isn't meant to give a full perspective and understanding of God, because for one, I can't, and two, it takes work and time, which we will get to withiin several chapters. This chapter is meant to be a launching pad to get you thinking about your perspective of God.

So, let's launch! He will reveal areas where your perspective needs to change as we go through this book. But there are some specific attributes regarding the Father which are simply who He is. This list is not a complete list of the majesty of God, but it's a good place to start changing or gaining a clearer perspective.

God is sovereign—He is supreme over all. He is omniscient—He knows everything from beginning to end. He is omnipotent—He possesses unlimited power. And He is omnipresent—He is present in all places at all time. You cannot escape Him, nor hide from Him. He is unchangeable, unshakable, immovable, and undefeatable. He is righteous, just, and holy. He is the I AM. And He IS love (1 John 4:8). Did you catch that? God IS love. He didn't invent love; love is His nature. He doesn't sparingly give love; love flows from Him. He doesn't demand to be loved; He is love at its fullest. He desires us to love Him, because He first loved us (1 John 4:19). Our love brings Him joy, but if we choose not to love Him, it doesn't deplete His love, nor does it cause God to withhold His love from us. God IS love in love's purest and most beautiful, joyful, complete form (1 Corinthians 13:4-8).

In 1 John 4:8, the word love comes from the Greek words **agan** *(much)* and agape *(to love, feast of love, a dear love)*. Their meanings are rooted in the Hebrew word **'âgab,** pronounced **aw-gab,** which is a prime root meaning *to breathe after, to love, to dote.* God breathes after us. He excessively, extravagantly loves us.

Love is who He is. Love is His essence. Love is His heart. Love is His nature and embodies His character. Love dictates every decision He makes. And He loves you!

I may challenge some people's theology here, but I propose that God's love for you, as His created child, never diminishes regardless of your actions. There is nothing you can do to make Him love you more or less. Even if you choose not to believe and accept Jesus Christ as your Lord and Savior, Father God still loves you. His love for you is unconditional (John 3:16, Romans 5:8, Ephesians 2:4).

However, entering His Kingdom, being able to live out His promises, and having eternal life is conditional. There is one condition. You must confess with your mouth and believe in your heart that Jesus Christ is Lord.

I find it interesting that God had one condition for Adam and Eve to remain in the Garden of Eden. Then, thousands of years later, God gave us one condition to have a hope and a future. One choice brought destruction. One choice brings abundant life. The Heart of the Father; keep it simple.

For those who are battling in their minds about the commands and instructions of God, we'll get into those later. Right now, it's about His heart. Because once you have the right perspective regarding the heart of God, you can better understand His commands. They take on a whole different perspective, because you know the motive behind them is love, not manipulation or control.

So what is love? Depending upon where your perspective of Father God is, His love is revealed throughout creation and His Word. Sometimes, in the chaos of the world, it can be difficult to see—but His love is always there. It can always be found, if you choose to see it.

From Genesis through Revelation, the love of God is evident and overwhelming. However, 1 Corinthians 13 gives us the most beautiful description of love ever written. If you're like me, when I first read this list, I thought it impossible. I cannot love like this. But when unadulterated love is continually flowing from the Father to me, I can absolutely love: maybe not perfectly, but I can keep aspiring to become a person who genuinely loves like this.

> *"Love endures long and is patient and kind; love never is envious nor boils over with jealousy; is not boastful or vainglorious, does not display itself haughtily. It is not conceited—arrogant and inflated with pride; it is not rude (unmannerly), and does not act unbecomingly. Love [God's love in us] does not insist on its own rights or its own way, for it is not self-seeking; it is not touchy or fretful or resentful; it takes no account of the evil done to it—pays no attention to a suffered wrong. It does not rejoice at injustice and unrighteousness, but rejoices when right and truth prevail. Love bears up under anything and everything that comes, is ever ready to believe the best of every person, its hopes are fadeless under all circumstances and **it endures everything** [without weakening]. Love never fails..."* (1 Corinthians 13:4-8a, AMP, emphasis added)

Let's read those same verses again with a few word substitutions:

> *"God endures long and is patient and kind; He never is envious nor boils over with jealousy; He is not boastful or vainglorious, and does not display Himself haughtily. He is not conceited— arrogant and inflated with pride; God is not rude (unmannerly), and He does not act unbecomingly. God does not insist on His*

*own rights or His own way, for He is not self-seeking; He is not touchy or fretful or resentful; and He takes no account of the evil done to Him—pays no attention to a suffered wrong. God does not rejoice at injustice and unrighteousness, but He rejoices when right and truth prevail. He bears up under anything and everything that comes, He is ever ready to believe the best of every person, His hopes are fadeless under all circumstances and **He endures everything** [without weakening]. Father God never fails..."*

There you have it: the Heart of the Father—Love. Oh, how beautiful You are, oh Lord!

As we delve into these wondrous words, I pray that your perspective of the Father's heart will shift in such a way that it transforms your relationship with Him, positively changing how you see yourself, value others and appreciate the world around you. I pray you will see all things through the looking-glass of love.

As we go through each precept, I'll bring in another verse from the Word of God. It is my hope that, as God reveals His heart to you, your revelation regarding the referenced verse will shift to a higher perspective... a crystal-clear, love-inspired perspective.

   • **God endures long and is patient and kind;**
   "The Lord is not slack concerning His promise, as some count slackness, but is longsuffering toward us, not willing that any should perish but that all should come to repentance." (2 Peter 3:9)

We often grow impatient at the state of the world we see. We begin to think things like 'There is no God,' or 'He doesn't care,' or 'Why doesn't Jesus come back now?'—all kinds of things which make us question Him and His truths. But God sees from an eternal perspective. He is not slow. He is holding back the reality of His final plan of full restoration because He doesn't want even one to perish.

   • **He never is envious nor boils over with jealousy;**

When you first read the verse below, the first thought you'll probably have is something like, "It sounds like God was a little envious and jealous in this situation." First, at minimum, read the verses before and after to put things in a more accurate context. Second, when Scripture is telling a 'story,' read the entire story. It will give you a better picture of why things happened. Always, put on the 'heart of love' perspective and remember, God is Sovereign.

7

"For the LORD your God is a consuming fire, a jealous God."
(Deuteronomy 4:24)

Envious is easy to put into the right perspective. There is no reason for God to be envious. There is no true and living God but Him. All other things man choses to serve, worship or call god are false, counterfeits, or man-made.

Jealous takes a bit more to delve into. But I love having to do this because it provides the opportunity to turn to the Father and ask Him, which builds a stronger relationship between us. *Jealous*, defined as suspicious; apprehensive of rivalry; uneasy through fear that another has withdrawn or may withdraw affection; suspicious that another is more loved or respected than ourselves. For me, this definition doesn't fully align if God is love. Also, if He is truly an Almighty God, which I believe He is, it doesn't fully align that He'd be 'apprehensive of a rival.' So, I need to seek further.

Jealous can also mean to defend the honor of; concerned for the character of; anxiously careful and concerned for. Okay, we're getting closer to something I can wrap my mind around. And it appears it's going to be a combination of the two.

Processing the foundational perspective that God is love, here is the revelation and understanding the Holy Spirit has led me to. The Lord God is the one and only living God. He is the Creator of life and all things; therefore, He has the right to demand His rightful place of first in our lives. However, because He is love and not a dictator, He sets before us the right to choose. He spells out for us what happens when He is first and we follow His commands, and what happens when we don't. If we choose to set a god before Him, He allows it, because of the free will He has given us. But He will not relinquish who He is; therefore, He will not take a second seat to anyone or anything. He will not tolerate a so-called rival in His creation's life, even if it's to accommodate His own creation's choice which He has given us. Why? Because forcing someone to love you isn't love.

He is love, and He is a jealous God over who and what is rightfully His. He will never stop being concerned over you. He will relentlessly give you every opportunity to experience His faithfulness and goodness so you will choose to be in the right relationship with Him. But take heed: God is quite clear on the consequences one will endure should they continually choose to rebel against or mock Him. We may have difficulty reconciling our understanding of love with this Truth, but His consuming fire will devour those who, once again, CONTINUALLY choose to reject Him and His commands. He is still love.

8

- **He is not boastful or vainglorious, and does not display Himself haughtily.**
"And he [Moses] said, 'Please, show me Your glory.'"
(Exodus 33:18)

God revealed Himself to Moses in different ways, but none of them in an arrogant way. Moses knew there was more to God, so he asked God to reveal Himself more. If God was a boastful god, He could have displayed Himself in the most flamboyant of ways. Yet He chose to display Himself in ways that would draw Moses closer to Him, rather than push Moses away.

- **He is not conceited—arrogant and inflated with pride;**
"And God said to Moses, 'I AM WHO I AM.' And He said, 'Thus you shall say to the children of Israel, "I AM has sent me to you."'"
(Exodus 3:14)

This part of the story almost contradicts God not being boastful. God isn't being boastful or arrogant here; He simply states the Truth of who He is.

- **God is not rude (unmannerly), and He does not act unbecomingly.**
"Then the Lord God called to Adam and said to him, 'Where are you?'" (Genesis 3:9)

God knew exactly where Adam and Eve were and what they had done. But rather than swooping down on them and immediately reprimanding them, He engaged them in a conversation.

I encourage you to read the second and third chapters of Genesis to gain a clearer perspective on what has led up to this part of the story. Here is a quick overview of what has transpired thus far. God created man and woman. He put them in a Garden paradise, where they had everything they could ever need. He gave them one rule: "...but of the tree of the knowledge of good and evil you shall not eat, for in the day that you eat of it you shall surely die" (Genesis 2:17). He told them the consequence if they chose to ignore His Word.

They ate.

God was walking in the Garden for their customary evening conversation. And from Genesis 3:9, by God's question, it would appear God couldn't find Adam and Eve. But Almighty God didn't lose them; He knew exactly where they were and what they had done. He was giving them an opportunity to tell the truth and own up to their choice.

If He were not who He is, He could have quite easily appeared immediately in front of them. He could have also berated, beat down, yelled or screamed at, and even zapped them out of existence. Yet He simply asked them questions and explained, once again, the depths of the consequences of their choice, then allowed the truth of what He had told them to unfold. You may be asking yourself why He didn't just give them a second chance. I'll let you seek a portion of the answer out with the Lord, if you so choose. The remainder of the answer is revealed later in Genesis 3, verses 22-24.

There was a second tree in the Garden, the Tree of Life. If they ate of that tree, they would live forever. God loved Adam and Eve too much to allow them to perpetually live in the state their disobedience had created: afraid, naked, ashamed, hiding, fully knowing good and evil.

- **God does not insist on His own rights or His own way, for He is not self-seeking;**
  "I call heaven and earth as witnesses today against you, that I have set before you life and death, blessing and cursing; therefore choose life, that both you and your descendants may live..." (Deuteronomy 30:19)

God has every right to forcibly insist on His own way or demand His own rights be enforced. Yet, because He is love, He lays out Truth for people to use the mind and the heart He created to willingly choose— life or death. His heart is once again revealed in His hopeful answer, *'therefore choose life'*.

- **He is not touchy or fretful or resentful;**
  "God said, 'I forgive them, honoring your words. But as I live and as the Glory of God fills the whole Earth—not a single person of those who saw my Glory, saw the miracle signs I did in Egypt and the wilderness, and who have tested me over and over and over again, turning a deaf ear to me—not one of them will set eyes on the land I so solemnly promised to their ancestors. No one who has treated me with such repeated contempt will see it.'" (Numbers 14:20-23 THE MESSAGE)

In these verses, God had recently brought the Israelites out of slavery through miraculous ways. He had had their masters load them up with gold and other riches. They had witnessed Him creating a dry passageway through a sea. He had guided them through the miraculous, including leading them by a cloud and a pillar of fire. These people had seen with their own eyes such wonderous things, yet they didn't believe or trust that He was enough to give them the land HE HAD PROMISED to GIVE them.

I personally believe that they *refused* to trust Him. They were too afraid to break off the bondage of slavery and quit living as victims. God knew their fears, and He showed them His power and goodness time and time again. They still chose bondage. So, with a heavy heart, God allowed them to live out the consequences of their choice and die in the wilderness, never to enter His promise. And they were just one step away from entering in! Heartbreaking. But don't we, too often, do the very same thing?

- *He takes no account of the evil done to Him—pays no attention to a suffered wrong.*
  "For I will be merciful to their unrighteousness, and their sins and their lawless deeds I will remember no more." (Hebrews 8:12)

Time and time again, Israel violated God's covenant with them. Basically, they did God wrong and did great evil against Him. Yes, He allowed them to go through consequences, hopefully to learn from their mistakes. But God, time and time again, operated in grace, including bringing to fruition His New Covenant through Jesus Christ, which He promised back in Genesis 3.

- *God does not rejoice at injustice and unrighteousness,*
  "Arise, go to Nineveh, that great city, and cry out against it; for their wickedness has come up before Me." (Jonah 1:2)

God told his prophet Jonah to warn Nineveh that if they didn't turn from their wicked ways, destruction was coming their way. Jonah didn't want to go because he despised the Ninevites, and personally became their judge. Through a series of events, Jonah went and warned Nineveh. Then, through a choice made by the king of Nineveh for all the people, they believed God and repented. The entire city was saved.

God does not rejoice at injustice and unrighteousness. Instead, He provides every opportunity for individuals, and even entire cities, to turn from evil and wickedness.

- *He rejoices when right and truth prevail.*
  "Yes, I will rejoice over them to do them good, and I will assuredly plant them in this land, with all My heart and with all My soul." (Jeremiah 32:41)

God, since the beginning, has spoken and revealed truth to people. Through encounter after encounter, experience after experience, He has displayed the contrast between following Him versus following self or others. His focus is to love, restore and to rejoice over them. He desires to DO THEM GOOD with all His heart and soul.

- ***He bears up under anything and everything that comes,***
"Now therefore, heed their voice. However, you shall solemnly forewarn them, and show them the behavior of the king who will reign over them." (1 Samuel 8:9)

Israel rejected God's leadership and demanded a king be set over them. So God said, "Okay, if that's what you want," and allowed them to have a king set over them. But, out of His goodness, He told His prophet Samuel to warn them beforehand what it would be like to have a king. (Read 1 Samuel 8:10-18.) Despite the warnings, Israel wanted to be like every other nation, and a king was selected.

Taxes, penalties, and heavy burdens soon became the norm. And they became even more burdensome as king after king built their personal kingdoms. It happened just as God had said it would. God then waited; the people cried out and He answered, because He loves.

- ***He is ever ready to believe the best of every person,***
"For I know the thoughts that I think toward you, says the Lord, thoughts of peace and not of evil, to give you a future and a hope." (Jeremiah 29:11)

God is speaking directly to His prophet Jeremiah. He is encouraging Jeremiah in the calling He has called him to. He speaks this over each of His people still today. He has a future and a hope for you. He thinks thoughts of peace towards you. Remember, He is love.

- ***His hopes are fadeless under all circumstances***
"...I am determined to do good..." (Zechariah 8:15)

God Himself says He is determined to do good. He has a firm and fixed purpose to do good, to bless. Then, He says, don't fear. And, in the following verses, 16-17, He tells us how He wants us to live: tell the truth, do the right thing by one another, don't take advantage of others, keep your lives simple and honest. Does that sound like He doesn't want the best for all people?

- ***He endures everything*** *[without weakening].*
"'And I will establish My covenant with you. Then you shall know that I am the Lord, that you may remember and be ashamed, and

never open your mouth anymore because of your shame, when I provide you an atonement for all you have done,' says the Lord God." (Ezekiel 16:62-63)

Ezekiel 16:1-59 lays out all the consequences that God's people will endure for generation after generation of rebellion against Him. Then, out of hope and love, He says "nevertheless". His hope and love is an everlasting covenant. His atonement was, and is, His Son, Jesus Christ.

- **Father God never fails..."**
"For God so loved the world that He gave His only begotten Son, that whoever believes in Him should not perish but have everlasting life." (John 3:16)

The Words from Scripture hold power, transforming power, because God backs them up. But the effectiveness they have in your life is only to the degree you *allow* them to work in your life. It, again, is the gift and responsibility of free will. It has been my experience that God will provide/allow a situation to occur for His truths to come alive in one's life. Many times we justify it as coincidence, but it is not. It is an opportunity to see and experience His heart.

His heart is love.

Right now I'm going to take a detour, and it might seem as though I'm going to contradict everything we've gone through thus far. Bear with me. Throughout Scripture, you are going to encounter great acts of violence, atrocities, times of anger, seemingly unfair consequences for minor infractions, even forsaking of beloved ones, all committed or allowed by Almighty God.

Even in these situations, I see the underlying, overwhelming love of God. Ever since man and woman's first rebellion, God has been displaying, for all who want to see, what life could be with Him versus what life becomes without Him. Ever since the beginning, God has been relentless in restoring mankind to his originally created state, in perfect communion with his Creator.

Jesus Christ said it in Matthew 18:14, *"Even so, it is NOT THE WILL of the Father who is in heaven that ONE OF THESE SHOULD PERISH."* (emphasis added)

God's heart is that not one person should perish. Unfortunately, to His sorrow, people choose to perish, rather than choosing to enter His promise.

Everything flows from His love, joy and peace. All flows from His patience, kindness, faithfulness, gentleness, and self-imposed control. Life flows from His goodness—for that is His Heart.

This book is based upon and written from the only true perspective: God IS love. And He LOVES you. Any other perspective is a distortion of truth, and provides an unstable and unsustainable foundation from which to live and govern your life.

Every self-view, thought, opinion; worldview, action, reaction; knowledge, understanding, etc., must be processed through God's love for you. As you align yourself with God, His heart, His ways, you will be transformed into who you were destined by Him to be. It is the greatest journey of your life. God desires for you to be made free.

Let freedom prevail in your life!

CHAPTER 2

Jesus Christ, Redeemer

"Stand fast therefore in the liberty by which Christ has made us free, and do not be entangled again with a yoke of bondage."
(Galatians 5:1)

Genesis 1-3 tells the story of our creation. It's a source of great debate, and sadly, used to try and discredit the value of who we are and are designed to be. I'm not going to defend the first three chapters of Genesis. You can work that out with God. He is big enough to handle your respectful questions.

I'm also not going to argue about timelines, logistics, or minute points that, in the big scheme of things, have no bearing. We are challenged individually to work out our own salvation with fear and trembling (Philippians 2:12). Again, I encourage you to work it out with God, with respect and a genuine heart to understand. I believe He enjoys this type of seeking.

I am going to present the portion I believe God wants us to know that is relevant to the intent of this book. You were made to be free.

You were not created with the intent of knowing evil. God planted two trees in the Garden of Eden. The Tree of Life gave eternal life. The Tree of Knowledge gave the ability to know evil. If God had wanted us to know evil, He would have given us the knowledge of it from the beginning.

You were not created with the capacity to carry the weight of evil. God commanded man not to eat of the Tree of Knowledge. But He didn't command him not to eat of the Tree of Life. So God wasn't concerned about man living forever. He was concerned about His creation knowing and carrying evil.

There are endless debates and discussions about the trees, the fruit, the serpent. Don't let those discussions overshadow nor distract you from the intended meanings of the story. God created man with free will. God commanded man not to do one thing. God told man the consequences of what would happen should man not trust God's Word and disobey. There is a real enemy. God's creation chose to believe the enemy over their Creator. And the consequences that God said would occur occurred. It was Truth then, it is Truth today, and will continue to be Truth forevermore. God's Word is trustworthy.
God told man if he ate of the Tree of Knowledge, he would surely die. When man and woman chose to eat, and their eyes were opened to evil, they died from their original created state. Eventually, they died physically.

We will get into this in a bit more depth later, but I want to give you something to begin to think about. Lying is an evil—a sin. We, unfortunately, have become numb to lies. It's become an acceptable part of society. But its damage to our being is far-reaching, in some ways we realize and many we don't. But God knows.

Think back to the first time you can remember being lied to by someone you cared about. Dig deep and remember how you felt. What did it do to your heart? How did it change how you felt about that person? How did it affect other or future friendships/relationships? Being lied to wounds us and has the ability to harden our heart, will and spirit.

In the big scheme of life, lying, on the scale of sin, is a 'small' thing. But think of the damage one seemingly small sin does to you and others. Now, for a moment, think about another sin: stealing. Has someone ever stolen something from you? Did you feel violated, betrayed? Did it create great mistrust of others? Did it wound your heart?

Evil is a heavy burden. God did not want us to ever carry its weight.

You were not created to live in the bondage evil produces. Genesis 3:22 reveals God's heart on why he removed man from the Garden: *"Behold, the man has become like one of Us (Father, Son, Holy Spirit), knowing (how to distinguish between) good and evil; and now, he might stretch out his hand and take from the tree of life as well, and eat (its fruit), and live (in this fallen, sinful condition) forever"* (AMP).

16

Evil puts us into bondage. God never desired us to live in the bondage evil produces.

Bondage, slavery or involuntary servitude; captivity, imprisonment; restraint of a person's liberty (1828 Webster Dictionary).

Let's get real here and turn the tables a bit. Think back to a situation when you lied to someone. What was the first thing you felt? Did it keep nagging you? If you didn't correct the lie, what did you think and feel every time you saw the person? Did you have to keep lying to cover up the original lie? How did it affect your relationship with the person? How did it affect how you engaged in other relationships? Was fear of being found out constantly knocking on your heart?

One lie, one evil, put you into a place of captivity to the lie and imprisoned you to the domino effect of consequences. It restrained you from engaging in an open and honest relationship because you chose to break the bond of trust, even if at the time, the other person didn't know it.

When the lie was exposed, did you see the pain in the other person's eyes?

While there are numerous purposes of the Old Testament of the Word of God, two really stand out to me. The Old Testament is a revelation of God's definition of sin, contrasting the consequences of living according to God's principles or the world's, which includes your own worldly desires. But, most importantly, the overarching purpose of the Old Testament in the Word of God is to reveal God's plan of redemption.

Jesus Christ steps into humanity.

At the opportune moment, God interrupted the timeline of humanity with the birth, life, death and resurrection of His Son, Jesus Christ. Jesus is the fulfillment of God's plan to redeem mankind from the consequences set in motion by man's (and woman's) decision not to trust God at His Word.

Redeem, to purchase back; to ransom; to liberate or rescue from captivity or bondage, or from any obligation or liability to suffer or to be forfeited, by paying an equivalent (1828 Webster Dictionary).

Jesus Christ redeems those who choose to confess with their mouth and believe in their hearts that He is Lord.

God created humanity with the extraordinary, but complicated, gift of free will. He did not create us to be mindless robots. His heart was for His creations to learn, grow, and engage in a meaningful relationship with Him. God's heart has never been to force us into a relationship with Him. He has given and will continue to give us the freedom to choose—even though He knows it's to our detriment when we don't choose Him or His Son.

God confronts sin (unrighteousness, evil, unholiness, whatever you'd like to call it). Always. Because, again, He knows sin destroys. In that confrontation, you are given two, and only two options: repentance or rebellion. There is no grey area on this.

Repentance, sincere remorse; sorrow or deep contrition for sin, as an offense and dishonor to God, a violation of his holy law, and the vilest ingratitude towards a Being of infinite benevolence.

Rebellion, an open and avowed renunciation of the authority of the 'government' to which one owes allegiance; open resistance to lawful authority.

As I mentioned, the Old Testament contrasts following God verses rebelling against Him. It also reveals the outcomes when the choice was repentance or rebellion.

- Nineveh, when told by the Prophet Jonah that they would be overthrown in forty days, chose to believe God; they repented of their wicked ways and they were saved (Book of Jonah).

- Sodom and Gomorrah were just as wicked as Nineveh, but they were destroyed because not even ten righteous men could be found in Sodom (Genesis 18-19).

- The ten men who spied out the Promised Land and rebelled against God's Word that He had given them the land died of a plague. And the people, an entire generation, who believed them instead of the Lord died in the wilderness. They never entered the promise of God (Numbers 14).

- The remaining two men, Joshua and Caleb, who believed the Lord ultimately entered the Promised Land, received blessings and lived long lives (Numbers 14).

Repentance always leads to restoration. Rebellion always leads to destruction. Undeniable truth.

The Ten Commandments given by God to Moses set the standard to which we are to live. Not adhering to them requires sacrifices to atone for the sin in order not to endure destruction or the wrath of God. The justice of God based on Law. I ask again, have you ever lied? Then you have sinned. You have rebelled against God and you deserve His wrath.

To not sin is an improbable standard.

But Jesus.

Jesus met God's standard; therefore, only He could pay the price for us to be made free from the curse of sin. He paid our obligation to God, so we would not be judged by God according to the Law's standard (Ten Commandments). He also died so we would have the opportunity to be restored to eternal life (Romans 6:14; Romans 3:21-26; John 3:15).

- God, in His love for us and knowing the penalty for rebellion is destruction and death, sent His Son to seek and to save that which was lost (Luke 19:10).

- God, in His love, sent His Son to save the world through Him (John 3:17).

- Jesus Christ, in His love for the Father, and for us, laid down His life of His own initiative to pay our price to be reconciled to the Father (John 10:17-18; Romans 5:10).

- Jesus Christ did not come to be served, but to serve, and to give His life as a ransom for many (Matthew 20:28).

I realize that using the words wrath and God in the same sentence may seem to contradict Chapter 1, *The Heart of the Father*. You must always keep in mind that God is God. He is sovereign. He is holy. There is no other. He is loving, kind, good, merciful, full of grace. He is holy, righteous, powerful, and the highest authority. He is also justice. And His justice is carried out according to His standard and His ways, which are higher than ours. The standard is the Law, The Ten Commandments. God gave them to us so we would understand how we should live.

You may be thinking that lying or stealing are small things compared to more violent acts of sin. Surely, if God is love, why would I need to be concerned about God's wrath when acts of violence are so much more than something as small as stealing? It's a vast discussion, and as your relationship with God grows, He will give deeper revelations. So I'm only going to plant a seed here.

God is just. He, and He alone, determines the justice each of us deserves.

Justice, the virtue which consists of giving to everyone what is due, impartiality in its distribution.

God administers justice impartially, because He holds Himself, and us, accountable to the principles He governs by. This does not change the truth that He loves every single person on this planet, regardless of their choices. But it does mean that every single person will receive justice for their choices.

For those who CHOOSE to confess with their mouth and believe in their hearts that Jesus Christ is Lord, we are saved from judgment under the Law. We will be judged by God under grace, which is God's heart, otherwise He never would have sent our Redeemer (Romans 10:9, 6:14, 6:15). Those who choose to reject Jesus Christ as their Lord and Savior will be judged by the Law (Romans 2:12).

The choice is, as it has always been and always will be, ours.

Always remember, it was Father God who, out of His tremendous love for us, sent His Son Jesus Christ to set us free from the Law. His heart isn't to judge us by the standards of the Law, but He will based on our accepting or rejecting of Jesus Christ as Lord. His heart is able to judge from grace. As in the Garden, God gives man the right to choose.

Jesus Christ is the Way, the Truth and the Life. There is no other way to be reconciled to Father God and live under grace than through believing in Jesus Christ. There is no other way than through Jesus Christ and the work He finished on the Cross to break the curse of sin and the bondage it holds us in. There is no other way other than through Jesus Christ and His work on the Cross to live in the promises and blessings of God.

Jesus made us free. He set us free from the Law. He set us free from the curse of sin. He set us free from curses. He set us free from death. He made us a new creation (2 Corinthians 5:17). We will delve into this Truth more later.

This is great news! I believe in Jesus. I live under God's grace. I don't have to worry about God's wrath. I have eternal life. God is going to bless me regardless of what I think, what I do, what I say. I can just keep living life how I want to!

Nope.

> "...And do not be entangled again with a yoke of bondage."

When you accept Jesus Christ as your Lord and Savior, you accept the new way of life God DESTINED you to live. This new life, this 'made free' life, is defined by God, not you, me or anyone else. This new life requires a restored heart. It requires a new way of thinking. It requires a new way of behaving.

The liberty, the freedom, we have was bought at a very high, excruciating price. And when we do not take a stand in that freedom but allow ourselves to be entangled with a yoke of bondage again, we squander the freedom bought for us by Jesus Christ.

The yoke of bondage is rule-keeping (in the controlling and condemning sense), personal religious plans rather than God's, and serving your own self-interest rather than God's and that of others. Continuing to do any of these puts you back into bondage to the Law, and you remove yourself from grace.

The yoke of bondage is operating in a work-based mindset to earn something from God, rather than a faith-based mindset to trust Him for who He is. You will never be able to do enough to make God love you more. And you will never do anything that makes Him love you less.

But your faith in Jesus Christ is just the beginning of a lifetime dedicated to being transformed by God's love, goodness, and Truth. You will not inherit the Kingdom of God without committing yourself to His process.

Jesus Christ did not abolish the Law. He fulfilled it (Matthew 5:17-18). So we still shouldn't lie. We still shouldn't steal. We still shouldn't commit adultery. We still should have no other god before God. There are six more, but the New Covenant of grace sums them up like this:

> "Jesus said to him, '"You shall love the Lord your God with all your heart, with all your soul, and with all your mind." This is the first and great commandment. And the second is like it: "You shall love your neighbor as yourself." On these two commandments hang all the Law and the Prophets.'"
> (Matthew 22:36-40)

The Law was about love. Grace is about love. They are just from two, very different, perspectives. One was based on works, which God knew and has proven that we cannot attain. But even during revealing the consequences of not listening and obeying His truths, He always provided a path to redemption and restoration. God's final path to redemption and restoration is through Jesus Christ. There is no other way.

When you accept Jesus Christ as your Lord and Savior, you are immediately reconciled to God and made free. However, He knows it takes time to cultivate a faith-based, genuine, love-filled relationship with Him. And He is relentless in giving opportunities to build it and draw closer to Him.

You also do not immediately have the heart and mindset to keep yourself free. You still need to work through heart wounds brought on by your sins and the sins of others that have touched your life. You still need to have your mind renewed by God's Truth, so you think and act freely regardless of any circumstance.

The work Jesus Christ completed at the Cross was complete. When Jesus said *"It is finished,"* the fulfillment of the Law was finished. Work-based faith was abolished. Faith-based work began (James 2:18).

Jesus Christ gives us the perfect example of what it means to have a faith-based relationship and faith-filled-work lifestyle (Luke 2:49). He obeyed God's plan for His earthly life because He loved and trusted Him (John 17:4). Jesus Christ had faith in God and His plans, so He did the work God asked of Him, believing (faith) that God was working all things out for good. Without faith, it is impossible to please God (Hebrews 11:6).

> *"And He (Jesus) said, 'Abba, Father, all things are possible for You. Take this cup away from Me; nevertheless, not what I will, but what You will.'"* (Mark 14:36)

Read His Words from THE MESSAGE version:

> *"Going a little ahead, he fell to the ground and prayed for a way out: 'Papa, Father, you can—can't you?—get me out of this. Take this cup away from me. But please, not what I want—what do you want?'"* (Mark 14:35-36, THE MESSAGE)

His heart-wrenching plea to Father God meant He was in agony; He knew God could intervene at any time and spare Him from the brutality

He knew He was about to endure. But because He had a relationship so deep with the Father, He had the faith to suffer for God's higher plan.

You may be arguing in your mind, "But Jesus Christ is the Son of God — of course He had faith!" Look again at the humanity in His prayer. As the Son of God, He had more knowledge and understanding about the abilities, power, authority of God than we can imagine. Yet, as the Son of God, He still asked: "Is there any other way? Do I really have to endure this? Take it away, please, Papa!" A very human plea. Then faith…

"Nevertheless, not what I will, but what You will." I trust You, Abba Father. I trust that what You have asked me to endure will be worth it.

"…Who for the joy that was set before Him endured the Cross, despising the shame…" wait for it…*"and has sat down at the right hand of the throne of God."*

Jesus Christ is alive and well. He is seated at the right hand of the throne of God. He is interceding on our behalf. And He is waiting for the appointed time when God leans over to Him and says, *"The time has come for You to interrupt the timeline of humanity again."*

It is through the confession of your mouth that Jesus Christ is Lord, and the belief in Your heart that Papa God raised Him from the dead, that you are reconciled to God and you are made free.

Jesus Christ set the example of the life you are to live. And God expects nothing less than for those who proclaim to follow Jesus Christ to pursue living as Jesus lived.

I can almost hear the thoughts in your head. The memories of trying and failing before, excuses, doubts, fears. And I can tell you this. You *can* live in freedom! Not because I say so, but because God says so. He, out of His love for you, made a way. His name is Jesus.

God made the process simple. We're the ones who complicate it and make it considerably more difficult than it needs to be. We make it more difficult because we fail to commit ourselves fully to renewing our minds and allowing our hearts to be transformed through our relationship with Almighty God.

When we choose to believe in Jesus Christ, we are committing ourselves to a new lifestyle. God has an answer for every question you have. He has a process for handling every situation you will encounter, internally and externally.

He also provides the answer to heal every wound; overcome every challenge; persevere through every trial or tribulation. Wait! Hold up! You mean I will still have challenges, troubles and trials?! I thought following Jesus Christ would remove the difficulties! Nope—sorry to say, but for seasons of your life, things may get more challenging.

Jesus Christ Himself tells us we will have trials in this world, and we will also have tribulation simply for believing in Him (John 16:33). You will endure persecution to varying degrees depending upon the call of God upon your life. It will also depend upon how much you stand and live your life according to God's Word.

But as I said, God has an answer for every situation, every challenge, trial and every persecution you may face. You are never left to face anything alone (Psalm 9:10, 37:25). And you are never separated from His love (Romans 8:35, 38-39).

Learning to live as Jesus lived positions you to receive your inheritance as a son or daughter of God. Did you catch that? You are a son, a daughter of God. Our faith in Jesus Christ makes us children of God; if we are children of God, then we are heirs of God. Therefore, we are joint heirs with Christ (Romans 8:16-17).

Your inheritance includes living a life made free by Him. Free from guilt and shame. Free from condemnation and worthlessness. Free from oppression and fear. You have a hope and a future (Jeremiah 29:11). You have peace (John 14:14). You have power and a sound mind (2 Timothy 1:7). And God, through Jesus Christ, has so much more for you.

Jesus Christ is our example. It was He who made the way for our hearts to be transformed. Our heart is God's focus. For He knows that when our hearts are transformed by His love and Word, we are forever changed. When we cooperate with Him in this process, there is no good thing withheld from us (Psalm 84:11).

I am reminded of the story of the rich young ruler (Mathew 19, Mark 10, Luke 18). This young man knew he was missing something in his life. He ran up to Jesus Christ, knelt before Him, and asked how he might inherit eternal life.

Jesus listed a few of the Ten Commandments, to which the young man replied, *"Teacher, all these things I have kept from my youth."*
This next verse is gut-wrenching to me. Verse 21: ***"Then Jesus,***

looking at him, loved him, and said, 'One thing you lack: Go your way, sell whatever you have and give to the poor, and you will have treasure in heaven; and come, take up the cross, and follow Me.'" (emphasis added)

The young man, with sorrow, wasn't willing to pay the price for the life Jesus Christ was willing to offer him.

We are often like this young man. We want what Jesus Christ is offering, and we run up to Him and kneel at His feet.

We ask Him how we can receive a promise of His: eternal life, hope, worthiness, peace, understanding, fulfillment, joy, a reconciled relationship, whatever the promise we are pursuing is at that moment. Then when Jesus, God's Word, gives us the answer, we turn away in sorrow because we don't trust that what God has for us is better than what we have. We are unwilling to pay the price to receive more of the blessings and promises of God.

Through the letter of the Law, the young man claimed he had followed the commandments. All his boxes were checked. He was in bondage to work-based relationship. But Jesus Christ was looking at the heart of this young man. Jesus knew he was in bondage to his possessions. And He, with love, pointed out his heart issue and gave him the answer to be set free from material bondage and receive a true inheritance.

The rich young ruler chose his possessions… and the bondage they carried. I firmly believe that had the young man been willing to sell his possessions, Jesus would have either stopped him or said, "Well done, good and faithful servant, you were faithful over a few things, I will make you ruler over many things." This is an illustration of how Jesus, therefore God, reveals heart issues to us. He is concerned about your heart. He will reveal and help you deal with anything putting you in bondage or hindering you from all the freedom He has for you.

Run to Jesus Christ. Kneel at His feet. Ask Him your questions. Be willing to pay the price He sets before you.

Do not be sad regarding the instructions of Christ. Do not turn away from the freedom Christ offers. Do not return, full of sorrow, to your old way of believing, thinking or living. Do not allow yourself to be entangled with that bondage ever again.

Stand fast therefore in the liberty by which Christ has made us free — for whom the Son makes free is free indeed!

26

CHAPTER 3

The Holy Spirit, Spirit of Truth

"However, when He, the Spirit of truth, has come, He will guide you into all truth; for He will not speak on His own authority, but whatever He hears He will speak; and He will tell you things to come."
(John 16:13)

The Person of the Holy Spirit has probably been the topic of many heated debates, the source of many church and denominational splits, and least understood—therefore, often ignored or avoided—promises of God for a follower of Christ. The Holy Spirit is meant to be a part of our lives, every moment of every day.

He—and I use He because He is not an it, but a living being (1 Corinthians 2:10-11)—tells us: *"But God has revealed them to us through His Spirit. For the Spirit searches all things, yes, the deep things of God. For what man knows the things of a man except the spirit of the man which is in him? Even so no one knows the things of God except the Spirit of God."*

I choose to refer to Him as the Holy Spirit, not the Holy Ghost, out of personal preference. You can work out your preferred terminology with God. But be quite careful about denying the existence of the Holy Spirit and/or His relevance today (Matthew 12:31).

The Holy Spirit is the Spirit of the Living God.

Unfortunately, for so many followers of Christ, He has not been embraced as a part of our inheritance as children of God. Consequently, the role He was meant to play in our lives has not been nurtured and developed. Because of this, many of us are less equipped to grow in our relationship with Father God, and the renewing of our minds to think like Jesus is more difficult. Yes, it is possible to have the mind of Christ (1 Corinthians 2:16).

We often, and far too quickly, plateau in our faith far beneath the abundant life given to us by Jesus Christ and filled with evidence of God's faithfulness and the truth of His promises. We also become frustrated due to disappointment at failing to be made free and live free as promised by God. We, no matter how hard we try, go back to old ways of thinking and behaviors that keep us bound in a life of lack rather than abundance.

Our lack of understanding of the operation of the Holy Spirit has allowed manipulation and control of the church and God's people to occur. And, on the opposite end of the spectrum, He has been used by some as a justification for behavior contrary to the Heart, Will and Word of God. It has also allowed people to operate in disorderly and dishonoring behaviors.

Therefore, it is essential for the children of God, followers of Jesus Christ, to know who the Holy Spirit is and to understand His indispensable role in the Kingdom of God and His significance in our lives.

The Holy Spirit is the third Person in the Trinity. There is God the Father, Jesus Christ the Son (Redeemer), and the Holy Spirit. They each have distinct roles but are in perfect unity.

2 Corinthians 13:14 gives a beautiful depiction of the integration of the Trinity and how we are to interact and build a relationship with each Being.

> "The grace of the Lord Jesus Christ, and the love of God, and the communion of the Holy Spirit be with you all."

This verse acknowledges that the Father, Son and Holy Spirit are three unique individuals, but are One. They, together, are from whom all the blessings of God flow and from whom all the work of the Kingdom of God occurs.

Mathew Henry's Commentary explains the intricate workings beautifully: *"...The grace of Christ as Redeemer, the love of God who sent the Redeemer, and all the communications of this grace and love,*

28

which come to us by the Holy Ghost; it is the communications of the Holy Ghost that qualify us for an interest in the grace of Christ, and the love of God: and we can desire no more to make us happy than the grace of Christ, the love of God, and the communion of the Holy Ghost."

God loves us. He sent the Redeemer to save us. Jesus Christ lived and died for us and is now interceding for us. The Holy Spirit reveals to us the grace found in Jesus Christ. The grace we find in Jesus Christ exposes the love the Father has for us. God pours out His love upon us. It's an exquisite flow.

It is wise to look at Biblical truths individually as well as how they flow with the entirety of the Bible. It is unwise to take one verse and build an entire perspective or argument upon it.

> *"In the beginning God created the heavens and the earth. The earth was without form, and void; and darkness was on the face of the deep. And the Spirit of God was hovering over the face of the waters."* (Genesis 1:1-2)

There are two Beings referenced in these two verses. God, who created. The Spirit of God, who hovered.

> *"Then God said, "Let Us make man in Our image, according to Our likeness..."* (Genesis 1:26a)

There are three Beings referred to in this verse. Let **Us** make man in **Our** image. God the Creator. Jesus Christ the Redeemer. The Holy Spirit, the breath of God. Jesus Christ Himself references three distinct Persons in Mathew 28:19:

> *"Go therefore and make disciples of all the nations, baptizing them in the name of the Father and of the Son and of the Holy Spirit..."*

If the Holy Spirit wasn't relevant then, or now, Jesus would have no reason to mention Him in the same manner with which He referenced the Father and Himself. If the Holy Spirit's work was completed in the past, then why hasn't Jesus come back? The Holy Spirit is still at work today.

Galatians 4:6 reveals an interconnectedness to the Trinity and adds a wild card to the relationship... us.

"And because you are sons, God has sent forth the Spirit of His Son into your hearts, crying out, 'Abba, Father!'"

As believers and followers of Jesus Christ, we are God's sons and daughters. God sent the Spirit of His Son, which is in essence the Holy Spirit, into our hearts as a confirmation that we are children of the Most High God. We are not orphans. We are not alone. He has not abandoned us. He is our Father God. The Holy Spirit within us bears witness to this truth.

When we do not embrace the reality of the Holy Spirit, and do not partner with Him to pursue God and His Truth, the Spirit bearing witness to God becomes a war against Him. God has given us the free will, the right, to reject Him and live however we want. The Spirit is unrelenting in revealing God, so a war between the Spirit of God and the free will of humanity rages internally, then usually manifests outwardly—often resulting in great destruction to the individual and those around them.

You do not have to fully understand the Holy Spirit to be receptive to Him. But you do have to open yourself up to the truth of His existence, who He is and His role in your life in order to be made free. He can take it from there.

The Holy Spirit was with the Father and the Son at the beginning of creation (Genesis 1:26), and He will be there at the end of time (as we know it), calling all who will listen to the Lord (Revelation 22:17).

The Holy Spirit is the Spirit of Truth and He guides all to Truth. Not the world's truth, but God's Truth (John 14:17, 15:26, 16:13. 1 John 5:6).

This is His primary purpose: to bring Truth, and it integrates with His significance in our individual lives. The Holy Spirit reveals God's Truth to us. He reveals who God is, who Christ is, who He is, and He gives revelation and understanding regarding the Kingdom of God (1 Corinthians 2:10). The Holy Spirit also reveals the plans, purposes and Will of God for every person who seeks to find them (John 16:13).

Here is another way the Father, Son and Holy Spirit work together. The Father formed us. He breathed His essence into us and gave us life. We are infused with His Being. The Son redeemed and reconciled us to the Father. He gave us the living example of the life we are to aspire to live. The Holy Spirit empowers and guides us to live the life Jesus Christ revealed to us. He leads us into the Truth of how to live a life made free in Christ Jesus.

The Word of God describes who the Holy Spirit is and His work in God's

Kingdom, therefore in our lives. It is imperative in the life of a follower of Christ to embrace the person of the Holy Spirit. As Corinthians 2:14-16 tells us:

> "The unspiritual self, just as it is by nature, can't receive the gifts of God's Spirit. There's no capacity for them. They seem like so much silliness. Spirit can be known only by spirit—God's Spirit and our spirits in open communion. Spiritually alive, we have access to everything God's Spirit is doing, and can't be judged by unspiritual critics. Isaiah's question, 'Is there anyone around who knows God's Spirit, anyone who knows what he is doing?' has been answered: Christ knows, and we have Christ's Spirit."
> (1 Corinthians 2:14-16, THE MESSAGE)

We were created with a mind (more later). We were created with a body (more later). We were created with a spirit. So, in order for us to grow in the spiritual things of God, we must embrace the Holy Spirit in our lives. Without our spirit communing with the Spirit of Truth, spiritual matters don't make sense because we are unable to receive the revelation of them.

The Holy Spirit, the Spirit of Truth, also aids us, and the world, in many other areas of life. I'll list a few here, but it is by no means an exhaustive list of the work of the Holy Spirit.

- The Holy Spirit is a gift of God, and He is our Helper (John 14:16-17).
- He bears witness that we are children of God (Romans 8:14-16).
- The Holy Spirit draws people to God (Revelations 22:17).
- He is the Spirit of grace (Hebrews 10:29).
- He is the Spirit of wisdom, understanding, counsel, might, knowledge and the fear of the Lord (Isaiah 11:2).
- The Holy Spirit is also the Spirit of life, prophecy, adoption, holiness, revelation, and glory (Romans 8:2, Revelation 19:10, Romans 8:15, Romans 1:4, Ephesians 1:17, 1 Peter 4:14).
- Hope is also the work of the Holy Spirit (Galatians 5:5).

Now, let's get into the less comfortable and more confrontational work of the Holy Spirit.

> "Nevertheless I tell you the truth. It is to your advantage that

I go away; for if I do not go away, the Helper will not come to you; but if I depart, I will send Him to you. And when He has come, He will convict the world of sin, and of righteousness, and of judgment: of sin, because they do not believe in Me; of righteousness, because I go to My Father and you see Me no more; of judgment, because the ruler of this world is judged."

"I still have many things to say to you, but you cannot bear them now. However, when He, the Spirit of truth, has come, He will guide you into all truth; for He will not speak on His own authority, but whatever He hears He will speak; and He will tell you things to come. He will glorify Me, for He will take of what is Mine and declare it to you. All things that the Father has are Mine. Therefore I said that He will take of Mine and declare it to you." (John 16:7-15)

In these verses, Jesus is trying to prepare the disciples of His approaching physical departure. They, as we do, were having difficulty comprehending what Jesus was telling them. They had their own preconceived notions and their own agendas on how Jesus should establish His Kingdom—with them right alongside Him, of course, reaping earthly glory while destroying those they believed were their enemies.

"It is to your advantage that I go away..."

This must have been a difficult thing to hear, much less understand for the disciples. They had been with Him for approximately three years. They saw Him work miracles. He taught them like no one else had before. They had purpose with Him. If they had a question, He was right there to answer it. How could it be an advantage for Jesus to go away?

"...For if I do not go away, the Helper will not come to you; but if I depart, I will send Him to you."

It was advantageous for Jesus to depart so He could send the Holy Spirit as the Helper to continue the work He had begun on earth. Jesus Christ was contained in a bodily form. Therefore, He could only be in one place at a time. But the Holy Spirit, our Helper, is in all places, at all times. Since it was Jesus Christ who sent the Holy Spirit, there is perfect unity on what needs to be accomplished for the purposes of God.

He also told them what the Holy Spirit's work would be, individually and globally.

"He will convict the world of sin..."

This work of the Holy Spirit makes people squirm, go into denial, become defensive or quite angry. We previously discussed that it is God who defines sin. He did so in order for us to learn to avoid choosing behaviors that harm ourselves and/or others. He, and He alone, has the sovereignty, authority and power to determine what sin is. People may believe they have that right, but that argument runs out of common sense and logic quite quickly.

The Holy Spirit lets people know when they are making choices againstthe Will of God. People, if they are being honest with themselves, know when they are not making the right decision. There is 'something' inside of them telling them not to do it, and the still small voice will resonate with an internal peace. But we have been given the free will to ignore and override His counsel. If the choice is to consistently override His guidance by our free will, it becomes easier and easier to do so. But there are internal and external consequences to doing so, because God's Truth always prevails. Always.

The Holy Spirit convicts us all of the reality of sin, the consequences of choosing sin, and the destructive nature of sin. The destructive nature of sin reveals the necessity for a Savior.

"...and of righteousness..."

The desired hope of conviction of sin is to evoke a hunger for righteousness. Righteousness is a purity of heart and uprightness of mind. It is conformity to God's Truth and leads to the understanding of holy principles. Righteousness embodies justice, honesty, voluntary obedience to truth, and a genuine affection for God, self and others.

When we experience the destructive nature of sin, the Holy Spirit points us to repentance. Repentance is a change of mind caused by deep sorrow for something we've done that violates God's law and causes pain to self and others, but above all it dishonors God. When we repent, have a change of mind (and heart) regarding living outside of God's Truths, it can't stop there. It must be followed by action, a change in the way we think and feel. It creates a thirst for righteousness, causing us to make conscious decisions towards right living. This isn't right living by human standards, but God's and God's alone.

But wait—there is more. Because we are incapable of living 100%

sinless, 100% of the time, the Holy Spirit reveals to our minds and hearts, through our spirit, that we have been made righteous because of Jesus Christ. We cannot establish our own righteousness.

Our righteousness, our right standing before God, was bought by our Redeemer. So, through the revelation of the Holy Spirit, we are righteous before God by our faith in Jesus Christ. This truth should compel us to make decisions to live righteously.

"...And of judgment..."

The Holy Spirit will convict the world of judgment. God created us with a mind, capable of wondrous thoughts and ideas. He created us with a mind that has the ability to reason, to acquire sound judgment. Judgment, *the act or process of the mind in comparing ideas, to find their agreement or disagreement, and to ascertain truth.*

The excuses we use to justify behaviors will not hold up before God. The "I didn't know better, I couldn't help myself, they made me do it, I was told it was alright", are in sharp disagreement with the God-given ability, Holy Spirit conviction to judge... ascertain, to learn, to discover Truth. This is the type of judgement we are to engage in.

Christ expounds even deeper on the Holy Spirit's work in each area of sin, righteousness and judgment.

"...Of sin, because they do not believe in Me..."

The Holy Spirit convicts people of the sin of unbelief in Jesus Christ and the redemption He offers. Most people agree that murder is wrong (a sin), but they refuse to acknowledge that denying Jesus Christ as Savior is wrong (a sin). The Holy Spirit is relentless in revealing the Truth of what Jesus Christ accomplished and provided at the Cross.

It is the constant warring between the conviction of the Holy Spirit and a refusal to believe in Jesus Christ that prohibits people from entering the rest promised by God. The Holy Spirit brings the conviction that if they continue in their unbelief, they will endure the consequences of living in opposition to God and will ultimately encounter the wrath of God.

To deny, justify, or dull the pain of this truth, people turn to false idols or other methods (addiction, pornography, humanism) to ease the void that only God, through Christ Jesus, can fill. Others become depressed, bitter, angry and even violent in their attempts to justify their personal beliefs and choice to deny Christ Jesus.

Their efforts to accept a substitute for God will not prevail over the work of the Holy Spirit, nor diminish the truth that we need a Redeemer.

> *"...Of righteousness, because I go to My Father and you see Me no more..."*

The Holy Spirit convicts the world to ascertain this truth. Jesus Christ was the only righteous man able to redeem mankind and is now seated at the right hand of the Father, interceding for us.

Christ returned to the Father so that mankind would have to determine for themselves if He was the Savior or just a teacher or prophet. The question has always been, "Do you trust God?"

> *"...Of judgment, because the ruler of this world is judged."*

The prince of this world, satan, the enemy, has been judged. Jesus Christ defeated the prince of this world at the Cross. He broke the power of deception and destruction brought into the world by satan.

The Holy Spirit convicts us to judge the Truth of the power of the Cross and Jesus' victory over sin and death. We have been given the ability to learn the Truth and then decide.

Each life will be judged by the choice they made on how to live their life. Judgment by God will occur based on the choice to follow the prince of the world (rebellion against God), adherence to the laws of God without Jesus (I'm a good person by my standard), or by their adherence to their faith in Jesus Christ (I have been redeemed).

He sent His Son and through Him, sent the Holy Spirit. God has given the world every opportunity to ascertain truth. He will never violate His gift of free will to mankind.

And God will show no partiality in judgment.

> *"I still have many things to say to you, but you cannot bear them now."*

Even after three years with the disciples, there were many things Jesus Christ wanted to teach them. But in His wisdom, compassion and intimate understanding of what they were able to comprehend at that time, He withheld the knowledge until a more appropriate time. A time when they would be able to receive and understand it.

He is the same with us to this day. The Word of God and the Kingdom of Heaven is filled with mysteries, revelations, gifts, truths, wisdom, knowledge—the list continues. But we may not be ready to receive the revelation of them, much less be able to put them into practice in our lives.

The Holy Spirit is sent to say what needs to be said, when it needs to be said and when God knows we are able to embrace it. We can embrace it because we are secure in the love of the Father and we trust Him. We have been convinced that Jesus Christ is Lord and He sent to us the Holy Spirit.

> *"However, when He, the Spirit of truth, has come, He will guide you into all truth..."*

As the Spirit of Truth, He will guide us into all Truth. The Holy Spirit is our constant guide into all the Truth of God. When we allow the Holy Spirit to convict and then guide us, He guides our thoughts, words, and actions to align with Truth.

He not only guides us; He is our constant companion to aid us in every situation. He guides us INTO truth.

I refer to Mathew Henry's Commentary, for how he describes our Guide can only be through the revelation of the Holy Spirit.

> *"To be led into a truth is more than barely to know it; it is to be intimately and experimentally acquainted with it; to be piously (devoutly) and strongly affected by it; not only to have a notion of it in our heads, but the relish and savor and power of it in our hearts; it denotes a gradual discovery of truth shining more and more."*

I encourage you to read that several times. Let it seep deeply into you as the Holy Spirit reveals the richness of being led by Him INTO ALL TRUTH, the beautiful wonders of God's Truth.

"...A gradual discovery of truth shining more and more." This is part of your inheritance as a co-heir with Christ, and will become more evident throughout our journey together.

The Holy Spirit will also guide us into our purpose, calling and giftings in order to fulfill what God has ordained for us.

He will guide us into Truth. The Truth He guides us into will never contradict the Heart, the Will, nor the Word of God. His guidance will not do harm but will do good. He will not manipulate or control us, but He will bring freedom from lies, sin, destructive thoughts and behaviors. He will not keep you dependent or co-dependent on any counselor or person. He will always guide you to God's love and Christ. It will make you free in who God made you to be.

The Truth He guides us into will not bring confusion, doubt, anxiousness or fear. He will always cultivate love, joy, peace, patience, kindness, goodness, faithfulness, gentleness and self-control in your life.

> *"...For He will not speak on His own authority, but whatever He hears He will speak..."*

The Holy Spirit operates on the authority of Jesus Christ. Christ's authority was given to Him by Father God. Therefore, anything spoken by the Holy Spirit will align with the Will of the Father. There will be unity. And what the Holy Spirit speaks will resonate with the spirit within you, because, like it or not, the Truth of God resonates with something deep inside of us.

Yes, we may try to argue with or ignore what the Holy Spirit says. But He searches, hears and knows the deep things of God—so the truth He speaks will prevail... always.

> *"...And He will tell you things to come."*

The Holy Spirit will tell us of things to come that pertain to us individually and the Kingdom of God. To live in this type of intimacy requires continual communion with the Holy Spirit. As we allow Him to transform us into the image of Christ, we can be entrusted with things to come.

A wonderful thing about God's grace and His love for us is that even when we miss it, but we're still pursuing Him, the Holy Spirit gives us promptings about upcoming changes. He hasn't told me the fullness all at once, but for most of the changes in my life, I've felt the Holy Spirit trying to prepare me for them.

When I allow Him to do so, when the situation happens, I'm more equipped to remain in peace, confidence and trust that God is working all things to my good and His glory.

> *"He will glorify Me, for He will take of what is Mine and declare it to you. All things that the Father has are Mine."*

"Therefore, I said that He will take of Mine and declare it to you."

Everything, and I mean everything, the Holy Spirit does will glorify Christ. Glorify: *to praise, to magnify, and to honor in worship; to ascribe honor to, in thought or words.* And I'm going to add my own little addition to this definition—*to ascribe honor to, in thought, words* or actions.

We, through the guidance of the Holy Spirit, are to continue the work Jesus Christ began. This means that He was not sent by Jesus Christ into this world to lead us to build our own kingdom. All that the Holy Spirit will lead us to, and equip us for, will contribute to the advancement of the Kingdom of God.

He will help us become equipped for the work for the Kingdom. And He will reveal the gifts, spiritual blessings and the inheritance we have as co-heirs with Christ.

We worship God. We follow Christ. We are led by the Holy Spirit.

The Holy Spirit is a gift from the Lord. He is sent by the Father, through the Son, to us. As a gift, you must ask to be filled with the Holy Spirit. Why? Because again, God has given us free will. He has left the decision in our hands of whether we want to receive His gift of the Spirit.

Scripturally, there are a number of ways to receive the Holy Spirit. It starts with asking. In the book of John, chapter 14, Jesus spoke of His Father sending the Holy Spirit. In John 20, Jesus Christ breathed on the disciples and said, "Receive." In Acts 2, the Holy Spirit descended because the people were praying in unity. They were all filled with the Holy Spirit and began to speak with different tongues. In Acts 19, Paul laid hands on people, and the Holy Spirit came upon them.

Therefore, to receive the gift and power of the Holy Spirit, you ask, believe, and start listening for His voice.

How do you know you've been filled with the Holy Spirit? Above all, you believe. You have faith in God to send Him to you. God loves giving good, beneficial, productive gifts to His children.

> *"If you then, being evil, know how to give good gifts to your children, how much more will your heavenly Father give the Holy Spirit to those who ask Him!"* (Luke 11:13)

The initial evidence of being filled with the Holy Spirit includes speaking in other tongues and boldness in doing the work of the Kingdom of God.

> *"And they were all filled with the Holy Spirit and **began to speak with other tongues, as the Spirit gave them utterance.**"* (Acts 2:4, emphasis added)

> *"And when they had prayed, the place where they were assembled together was shaken; and they were all filled with the Holy Spirit, **and they spoke the word of God with boldness.**"* (Acts 4:31, emphasis added)

Other evidences include operating in the gifts of the Spirit. We will review these glorious gifts in more detail later.

> *"But the manifestation of the Spirit is given to each one for the profit of all: for to one is given the word of wisdom through the Spirit, to another the word of knowledge through the same Spirit, to another faith by the same Spirit, to another gifts of healings by the same Spirit, to another the working of miracles, to another prophecy, to another discerning of spirits, to another different kinds of tongues, to another the interpretation of tongues. But one and the same Spirit works all these things, distributing to each one individually as He wills."* (1 Corinthians 12:7-11)

The Holy Spirit is our Helper. We are not orphans, left alone to navigate this life alone. God has given us the Spirit of Truth to abide with us forever. He dwells with us and is in us… if we ask Him to come and fill us.

If you're still questioning the need for the Holy Spirit, I leave you with this thought.

> *"Then Jesus, being **filled with the Holy Spirit,** returned from the Jordan and was **led by the Spirit** into the wilderness."* (Luke 4:1)

Jesus Christ, Son of God, Messiah, King, was filled and led by the Holy Spirit. How much more do we need to be?

PART TWO

Reality Check: Work Is Required

"But we all, with unveiled face, beholding as in a mirror the glory of the Lord, are being transformed into the same image from glory to glory, just as by the Spirit of the Lord." (2 Corinthians 3:18)

We are being transformed INTO the same image from glory to glory. Whose image? Jesus Christ. That is God's relentless purpose: the transformation of our lives. He wants us to live in peace, purpose, and passion. He wants us to have joy, peace, and love. His heart is for us to know that we matter, we belong, and we are cherished. He wants us to know who He is and who we are.

God's desire is for all of us to have the same heart and mind as Jesus Christ. He has done the work to provide us the opportunity to live an abundant life. The rest of the work is up to us.

> Work, *to operate; to produce effects by action or influence.*
> Work, *to obtain by diligence.*
> Work, *to bring into any state by action.*

It requires work, diligence, to cultivate and produce a heart and mind like Jesus.

We often "try out" this Jesus thing when life isn't working out too well, or tragedy hits us. This usually makes our initial motivation to follow Christ from a place of desperation due to brokenness, pain, and disillusionment experienced in a fallen world. So when God "fixes" the situation, we too often get the mindset of "Thanks, God, I'll take it from here." This type of relationship is not what God desires with us.

He wants the type of relationship where our motivation to pursue Him is born from an ever-deepening relationship with Father God, compelled by the revelation of how deeply we are loved and developing the ability to return love to Him and to others.

It requires work. Too many people quit the transformation process before they allow God to complete the work within us. We can be confident He is willing to do His part, but we must do our part.

The work I am talking about has nothing to do with the legalistic mindset that says works are the way to earn your way into God's goodness.

> You cannot work hard enough to earn salvation.
> You cannot be perfect enough to earn righteousness.
> You cannot serve enough to earn grace.
> You cannot follow rules enough to earn holiness.
> You cannot do anything to earn God's love.

These kinds of work are called dead works, and they produce no good thing. They only produce frustration because they are impossible to achieve.

You choose to live life differently when you choose to follow Jesus Christ. If you just asked yourself 'Why do I have to live differently now?', I have one question for you. How was living life outside God's Truths working out for you?

For me, there is no other life worth living than one in the pursuit of the heart and mindset of Jesus Christ. I tried the other way; I won't ever go back to being that person.

I'm not going to sugarcoat the challenges you will encounter. First, life is simply challenging. Second, when you add believing in Jesus Christ to the mix, you just entered a new realm of challenges, naturally and spiritually. Third, salvation, believing in Jesus Christ, is just the beginning.

Transformation is required, and it takes work. If you're discouraged already, I encourage you to read the first three chapters of this book again. A life lived in the love of the Father, in His Truth, by His Spirit, is a blessed, victorious and abundant life.

Becoming a follower of Christ compels us—not out of dead works, but out of love—to learn how to believe, think, and act how He did and does. It's a transformation of our heart and mind to know who God is and who we truly are.

Transformation is the most challenging, and uncomfortable, process you will ever go through. It forces you to take a good, hard look at yourself. More often than not you'll want to give up, to question why. You may lose friends, be made fun of, and experience persecution to varying degrees.

But the beauty of being transformed, if you stay the course, is that you will have peace in the midst of chaos. You will have joy in sorrowful times. You will have strength in the challenges. You will have wisdom beyond what humankind could ever think. You will have hope in supposedly hopeless situations. You will be able to do things others say are impossible. And, above all, you will abide in a place of safety, belonging and love. Because you are never alone.

I look at it like this. Have you ever gone on a diet and quit after a short period of time? Old habits quickly return. Unhealthy food cravings come back with a vengeance; exercise periods become further apart. Then, before we know it, we quickly gain back the weight, usually flying right past the original weight we wanted to lose.

Why does this happen? Because your mind had not become accustomed to a new way of thinking about food and eating. Your body had not become accustomed to a new exercise routine, and a new weight level. So, as soon as you quit before the 'tipping' point, your mind and your body revert to old, known and comfortable ways.

Counseling. Education. Lessons. All these things are great, but if you do not put into practice what you learn, they will not become part of who you are. They will not overcome old muscle memory, because they aren't in place long enough to replace the old ways.

A life pursing a relationship with God requires putting into practice His truths and allowing them to become part of who we are. They begin to define who we are. They give us the perspective on how we are to view ourselves, others, and the world.

His Truths are the driving force in how we respond to life in every aspect. And the work to allow our hearts and minds to be transformed to think and act according to God's Truth is HARD WORK. Why?

It is easier to hate than it is to love.
It is easier to hold on to grief than it is to find joy.
It is easier to get lost in chaos than it is to live in peace.

It is easier to receive instant gratification than be patient.
It is easier to ignore needs than to be kind.
It is easier to compromise than to be good.
It is easier to quit than it is to be faithful.
It is easier to be hard than to be gentle.
It is easier to defend than to have self-control.
It is easier to hold on to bitterness than to forgive.
It is easier to build walls than build healthy relationships.
It is easier to hoard than to give.
It is easier to condemn others than to extend grace.
It is easier to blame others than to take responsibility.
It is easier to live how you want to live than live by God's standards.
It is easier to think you're in control than it is to trust God.

Until your life falls apart.

Or, worse, you come to the end of your life and you realize your life was lived not fulfilling its potential.

I read something like this quote when I was making excuses for not doing something I needed to do.

> *"There is nothing worse than coming to the end of your life and meeting the person you were meant to be."*

This quote confronted my attitude and my justifications, creating a choice that had to be made. I could continue to make excuses, or do the work to be transformed by a new way of thinking, and ultimately, I responded. I chose to be transformed, and I continually choose to be transformed every day.

God's Truth confronts. God's Truth demands a response.

> Confront, *to stand face to face in full view; to stand in front.*
> Confront, *to stand in direct opposition, to oppose.*

You can either yield to it, and it will transform your life; or you can deny it, and you will be at constant war with it. God's Truth does not yield to mankind's opinion. God gives us the ability to think and make decisions and even form our own thoughts, perspective, "opinions" on a matter. That perspective might even become so engrained in our mind that it becomes our individual truth.

44

But, if it doesn't align with God's Truth, it simply isn't absolute. And it will ultimately be proven incorrect. Every. Single. Time.

Truth is backed by God's absolute authority and power. Truth derived by man is backed by a limited being, with limited knowledge, understanding and experience. And man's truth only survives until another man's "truth" builds upon, replaces or discredits it.

For years it was thought the earth was flat. Yet, thousands of years ago, the Word of God referenced a round earth: *"sits above the circle of the earth,"* and *"He hangs the earth on nothing,"* or *"He drew a circular horizon on the face of the waters."*
Let's bring truth closer to home and look at some self- or man-inspired, so-called truth.

- "I can do anything I want."

God's Truth says, *"Do not be deceived, God is not mocked; for whatever a man sows, that he will also reap."* (Galatians 6:7)

- "It's my body—I can do whatever I choose to do with it."

God's truth says, *"Or do you not know that your body is the temple of the Holy Spirit who is in you, whom you have from God, and you are not your own?"* (1 Corinthians 6:19)

- "I'm not worthy of love."

God's Truth says, *"We love Him because he first loved us."* (1 John 4:19)

- "I've made too many mistakes."

God's Truth says, *"For I will be merciful to their unrighteousness, and their sins and their lawless deeds I will remember them no more."* (Hebrews 8:12)

- "You'll never amount to anything."

God's Truth says, *"For I know the thoughts that I think toward you, says the Lord, thoughts of peace and not of evil, to give you a future and a hope."* (Jeremiah 29:11)

- "You're not smart enough."

God's Truth says, *"For God has not given us a spirit of fear, but of power and of love and of a sound mind."* (2 Timothy 1:7)

I could go on and on, replacing a temporary and shakable truth with God's eternal and unshakable Truth.

As a follower of Jesus Christ, you signed up to live differently. And in this new life, your reward is different than rewards given by man, and this world. Our rewards are far greater, and they are for now and for eternity. Be encouraged! You have the resources of heaven in your arsenal.

We often take *"I can do all things through Christ who strengthens me"* out of context. In the verses before, Paul says,

> *"I know how to be abased, and I know how to abound. Everywhere and in all things I have learned both to be full and to be hungry, both to abound and to suffer need. I can do all things through Christ who strengthens me."* (Philippians 4:12-14)

Paul **learned** how to 'be' regardless of his circumstances. God renewed his mind, which transformed his heart. Paul put the truth of God at work in his life and learned that the ebb and flow of life did not dictate his identity, peace or purpose.

The same is true for each of us. God wants to renew our minds with His Truths, commandments, to transform our hearts. The transformation of our hearts aligns us with God's heart, so we live in the abundant life Christ has given us.

The work is worth the results—I guarantee it. But don't take my word for it; take God's Word for it. Jesus said it best when He told the disciples, *"In the world you will have tribulation, but be of good cheer, I have overcome the world."*

Following Christ does not exempt you from having challenges or difficult times. But it does guarantee that you are not alone, and equips you with the mindset required to overcome them. So do not allow yourself to get discouraged. If God is for you, who can be against you?

Do not quit.

You are in training, and much like an athlete, you will hit a wall. You may want to give up, think that it's not worth the work. But, if you ask, God will give you a second wind, and you will suddenly find the strength to press on, and at top performance with less exertion.

God knows the result He has in mind for you, and it is glorious! He also knows how to get you there. So don't take God out of the journey, especially during the challenging times.

The results are worth the work. There isn't an athlete who doesn't feel an overwhelming sense of joy and accomplishment when they cross that finish line.
It is my prayer for you that the Holy Spirit will open your eyes so you may see the wondrous things of God's love and Truth.

Do the work—be transformed! Be made free!

CHAPTER 4

New Creation in Christ

"Therefore, if anyone is in Christ, he is a new creation; old things have passed away; behold, all things have become new."
(2 Corinthians 5:17)

This verse is one of the key verses in establishing and defining your identity found in Christ. 2 Corinthians 5:17 sets the defense to stand against every internal and external argument that comes against you, trying to convince you that you're never going to change. The truth and authority of this verse stands in direct opposition to the notion of "I couldn't help it," or "I just couldn't stop myself." It is your best defense against those who may say, "You'll never change."

"..If anyone is in Christ..." **If** and **in** hold substantial meaning in this verse.

If, εἰ, pronounced ei, is defined as conditionality. Conditionality is the quality of being conditional or limited. There is a limitation on the promise in this verse, held back by the requirement of terms revealed within it.

"...If anyone is..." If you have made the decision to follow Christ, then the promise of this verse holds true and there is not anything that anyone or anything can say or do against it. Not even you.

In, (be in), ἐυ, pronounced en, when traced back to its Greek origin means *fixed position*.

"...In Christ..." You are in Christ if you have taken up a fixed position in Him. You have chosen to lose your life in order to find your true life in Christ.

New, καινός, pronounced kahee-nos': recently made, fresh, unused, unworn, of a new kind, unprecedented, uncommon, unheard of.

Creation, κτίσις, pronounced ktis'-is, means original formation (properly, the act; by implication, the thing, literally or figuratively): building, creation, creature, ordinance.

If you have taken up a *fixed* position in Jesus Christ, then you are of a new kind. You have been made into your original formation. God reconciled you to Himself through the unprecedented act of love found in Jesus Christ.

This means you are no longer in bondage to incorrect thoughts about God, yourself, others, or the world. You are no longer oppressed by lies you've been told about yourself. You are no longer held hostage by past mistakes or destructive habits. It also means you have the capacity to see, think, feel and act from a higher perspective.

You have entered a new state of existence, where you are not subjected to pleasing others and fitting into patterns or molds that they, or the world, dictate you should adhere to. As a new creation, the only One you need to seek to please is God. This does not, in any way, give you permission to treat people in any other manner other than with respect, because a life lived in Christ goes full circle. This will become more and more evident as our hearts align with the heart of God and we are transformed by the renewing of our minds.

Through the life, crucifixion and resurrection of Jesus Christ, we have all been given the opportunity to be made new. Through the belief in your heart and the confession of your mouth that Jesus Christ is Lord, you are now a new creation.

Your highest priority as a new creation in Christ is to live your life the way God intended life to be lived. It is a life lived in close relationship with Him, with others and doing the work God calls you to. Jesus summed it up in Luke 10:27: *"So He answered and said, 'You shall love the Lord your God with all your heart, with all your soul, with all your strength, and with all your mind,' and 'your neighbor as yourself.'"*

Sounds simple enough, until you try to put it into practice. That is why we need the Holy Spirit. Remember, He is the one who leads us to all Truth. Truth with a capital "T," because it's God's Truth.

"But I still feel guilty, shameful, or unworthy." This is going to sound harsh, but Truth is not about how you feel. It is about what is TRUTH.

Unshakable, undeniable, immovable and eternal Truth backed by a power and authority that surpasses human limited understanding and capability.

Let's break this down a bit. I have a friend whose birth certificate says 'illegitimate.'

Illegitimate, *unlawfully begotten; born out of wedlock; unlawful; not genuine.*

'Illegitimate' defined who she thought she was for a long time. It was a foundational truth she processed everything in her life through. It was her perspective on how she viewed herself: unlawfully begotten; unlawful, not genuine. This perspective led her to believe that she was unwanted, unworthy, abandoned, unlovable, and so many other destructive and painful perspectives. It was how she thought others saw her. She processed everything through the truth that she was born out of wedlock.

It is true that my friend was born illegitimate, father unknown. But the Truth overrides that truth and the TRUTH is that, in Christ, she is a new creation. She has been adopted by her Heavenly Father. She is loved. She is wanted. She is worthy because this Truth is backed by the power and authority of One higher than a person, a piece of paper, and the world's viewpoint.

Man's personal truth is limited knowledge, processed through personal experience. Individual truth only extends as far as the next person agrees or disagrees with it. Humankind's truth is limited by the information we have been exposed to. It can be distorted and used to manipulate and control people. It can be used to keep people in bondage and to push forward individual ideologies.

As a new creation, God's Truth confronts anything that does not align with who He is, His Word and who He says you are. And God's truth says, if you are in Christ, you are a new creation; old things have passed away, all things have become new. Period.

You, through Christ, have been given a new heart and a new nature. You have also been given a new mind. Your body is to be treated with a new level of respect. This requires a new way of thinking, a higher way of thinking, perceiving and ultimately living. And, again, it's not based on how you 'feel'—it's based on who God is and who He knows you are meant to be.

God created us with emotions. They are meant for us to experience all aspects of life. However, they were never meant to be the driving force in our thought- or decision-making process. Emotions, when not tempered with reasoning and processed with the Holy Spirit, can lead us down paths that can put us in bondage and become destructive. Emotions can be fickle.

We live in a world so out of balance with the importance placed on individual feelings. It has caused great division, bitterness, fear, offense, isolation and hatred. One person's worth is trampled on because another person felt they had the right to do so, simply because they disagreed.

This is not the feeling, thinking and living of a new creation. Yes, I just said feeling. God does not want us to be emotionless robots. There will be times when you "feel" Him. You will "feel" His presence. There have been times when I've soaked in the beauty of a sunrise and I "feel" His presence so strongly it overwhelms me. Other times, I stopped to watch another glorious sunrise and I did not "feel" His presence as strongly. But I KNOW He is always with me. How do I know that? Because His Word tells me so. Therefore, it is Truth. It is not based solely on what I feel or even what I currently know. It's Truth because He says so.

You are going to feel all kinds of emotions as the Holy Spirit teaches you how to live as a new creation. Be mindful to align those emotions with the Truth of the Word of God. If you feel shame, allow yourself to feel it; ask the Holy Spirit why. The Holy Spirit will show you the godly way to deal with it. God will use the emotion of shame to bring repentance, healing and restoration. Shame is never meant to bring rejection of you—ever. But it is used to bring awareness to something you thought, or did, that is beneath you as a child of God.

God's Truth will always confront your heart, motives, thoughts, words, choices and actions. But His truth NEVER devalues you or another human's worth. EVER.

Remember, everything flows from the love of God, even correction, discipline, justice and the difficult circumstances we go through. That is the higher perspective the Holy Spirit will train you in.

As a new creation in Christ, old thoughts, old principles and old practices are going to be dealt with. While you have been immediately made a new creation, you still have some old ways of thinking and habits that hold you in destructive patterns. These destructive patterns, thoughts or actions limit you from receiving all God has for you.

It is difficult to put on paper the multifaceted ways God works all things to our good and His glory. He is always working through multiple ways to transform our character (heart, mind, body, nature). I'll start in a semblance of an order, but keep in mind that God works all things, through all circumstances, on multiple levels. You'll start to recognize

His hand the closer you two become.

You are reconciled to God because He sent His Son, our Redeemer. You have confessed with your mouth and believe in your heart that Jesus Christ is the Lord of your life. Therefore, you and God are no longer in a state of opposition. You have aligned your life to Him.

Did you catch that? *You aligned your life to Him*. He did not align Himself with how you live your life. He wants you to be transformed so you can live in His blessings, promises, and the inheritance He has for you. **He will not change Himself for you to live however you want.** He requires you to change into His image. Because that is how He created you to be.

He won't force you to change. He does not override His gift of freewill. But He will allow circumstances to arise in your life so you experience the contrast between living His way and living the world's way.

You have been given a new heart. Ezekiel 36:26 says, *"I will give you a new heart and put a new spirit within you, I will take the heart of stone out of your flesh and give you a heart of flesh."* Our hearts are hardened through the hurts, disappointments, wounds, and betrayals we experience in life. There are wounds we can trace back to a situation and know why we feel the way we do. There are often many wounds more difficult to trace back to an incident. It could be a series of events, or words spoken in haste or ignorance. These wounds can do more damage to our true identity because, either through our own justification or that of others, we convince ourselves it wasn't a big deal.

However, it planted a seed of doubt, mistrust, or confusion and put us into a place of self-preservation. That seed manifests itself in many ways throughout our life, often in ways we do not understand. Wounds come into our lives through varying circumstances. I've chosen divorce as an example, only because it has touched so many of our lives. Divorce has become so accepted that we fail to acknowledge, much less deal with, the known and unknown wounds in our hearts and identities caused by divorce. My parents divorced when I was young, and my first marriage ended in divorce. I am also married to a man who was divorced. So this example does not come from a place of judgement, but from a place of knowing that divorce wounds us, no matter the reason.

The effects of divorce and the breakdown of the family unit are evident. The permissibility of divorce has brought chaos, confusion, deep-seated anger and distrust, because children had to learn to adapt to environments God never desired for us. Hearts are knowingly and unknowingly hardened against God, marriage, fathers, mothers, and relationships because of self-preservation and a lack of security and structure needed in a healthy marriage and family unit. Children of divorce wrestle through guilt, confusion, abandonment, and self-worth and identity issues. Divorce leaves wounds not only in children, but in every life touched by divorce. This includes the one who initiates a divorce.

This example of the effects of divorce is by no means an argument to stay in an abusive marriage. If you're in an abusive marriage, seek professional help. Abuse is not God's heart.

The damage of divorce runs deep and through generations. Divorce is not the heart of God. In fact, He hates divorce. He hates it because it destroys families, an institution He created for safety, peace, and joy. He hates divorce because it destroys the emotional, mental, and spiritual well-being of His people.

But God is more than able to heal wounds inflicted by divorce or any other circumstance we've encountered. God has given us a new heart. God wants to heal every wound that has turned any piece of our heart into stone. If we don't allow God to heal our wounds, we carry them with us, and they weigh us down. We were not created to have hardened hearts. God wants our heart to be as His heart; a heart able to love and be loved.

You have been given a new mind. God created us with a mind able to process vast amounts of information, to comprehend, to form ideas and make decisions. He wants us to use our minds to govern (to regulate, to influence, to direct) our lives. He has given the responsibility to us of how to utilize our minds. This proves to be a challenging gift.

Many choose to use their God-given free will to fill their minds with degrees of violence, pornography, bloodshed, and other images and information that if continued will ultimately lead to their personal destruction. They will leave in their wake damage and wounds to those around them. I don't say so; God does. He gives many warnings about the destruction of a mind filled with things not worthy of who He created us to be. Jesus said it this way in Matthew 7:13-14: *"Enter by the narrow gate; for wide is the gate and broad is the way that leads to destruction, and there are many who go by it. Because narrow is the gate and difficult is the way which leads to life, and there are few who find it."*

So, just because the crowd says it's okay doesn't mean it's okay. If it goes against how God says we should govern our lives, then it will lead to destruction. People can argue, or justify, all they want. It will not change God's warning that the wages of sin are death.

We are not to be conformed to this world, but we are to be transformed by the renewing of our minds so that we will prove what is the good and acceptable and perfect will of God. We are to meditate (think) on things that are true, noble, just, pure, lovely, of good reports, virtuous and praiseworthy.

Challenging, yes. Impossible? No. We are a new creation in Christ; therefore, we have been given the ability to cultivate *"...the mind of Christ."* We do this through forming the habit of taking every thought captive and bringing it under the obedience of Christ.

You, through Christ Jesus, have within you the ability to take every thought captive and change how you think. You are no longer bound by thoughts that tell you you'll never amount to anything. That you're not good enough. You're not worthy. You'll never be forgiven. You'll never be able to be free of alcohol, drugs, pornography, or any other addiction such as shopping, excessive exercise, social media, overeating, undereating, debt—anything out of balance, therefore holding you in bondage.

"Thus says the Lord, your Redeemer, The Holy One of Israel: "I am the Lord your God, Who teaches you to profit, Who leads you by the way you should go" (Isaiah 48:17). The Lord teaches us how to profit. He teaches us how to live right and well. He shows us what to do and where to go. And it always leads to being made free. He leads us to be free from the destruction of a mind focused on all the wrong things.

We are a new creation in Christ; we choose to continually transform our minds to be like Christ. It's the more difficult way, but it leads to life. Always.

Your body no longer belongs to you. Your body belongs to the Lord. This is true for men and women. Romans 12:1: *"I beseech you therefore, brethren, by the mercies of God, that you present your bodies a living sacrifice, wholly acceptable to God, which is your reasonable service."* THE MESSAGE version says it like this: *"So here's what I want you to do, God helping you: Take your everyday, ordinary life—your sleeping, eating, going-to-work, and walking-around life—and place it before God as an offering. Embracing what God does for you is the best thing you can do for him. Don't become so well-adjusted to your culture that you fit into it without even thinking. Instead, fix your attention on God. You'll be changed from the inside out. Readily recognize what he wants from you, and quickly respond to it. Unlike the culture around you, always dragging you down to its level of immaturity, God brings the best out of you, develops well-formed maturity in you."* (Vs 1-2)

Every part of your life, including your body whether at work or play, is an offering to God. A new creation means every part of you is new. You cannot treat your body, your life, as the culture around us does. You are destined to a higher, better, healthier, more productive standard.

Our bodies are the temple of the Holy Spirit. *"Or do you not know that your body is the temple of the Holy Spirit who is in you, whom you have from God, and you are not your own? For you were bought at a price; therefore glorify God in your body and in your spirit, which are God's"* (1 Corinthians 6:19-20).

1 Corinthians 6:19-20 is not gender specific. Men and women are held accountable by God to this Truth. We, as new creations, need to be set free from the lie the culture of the world tries to convince us of regarding our bodies and our sexuality. Those who say "It's my body, I can do whatever I want to it" are following the wide and broad way, and it leads to destruction.

Destruction comes in many forms when we commit offense against our own bodies. The obvious are sexually transmitted diseases. The less obvious forms, when they are sexually intimate, are emotional and mental confusion, lack of trust and respect in relationships, and superficial encounters, damaging the ability to have healthy, balanced and fulfilling relationships.

Intimacy was designed by God to be a beautiful and fulfilling act between a husband and a wife, protected by the covenant of marriage. When sexual intimacy is taken outside of the marriage covenant, it causes insecurity and self-doubt in both men and women. It wounds and damages their God-given identity. Then it can grow into a complete lack of respect for one's self and members of the opposite gender. It creates a mindset that denies the respect of our and other's bodies, causing them to become an object. This mindset dilutes the beauty, vulnerability and trust of sexual intimacy and turns it into a base and animalistic act. Culture has, unfortunately, tolerated or encouraged men to pursue sexual encounters outside the covenant of marriage. Today, this cultural encouragement has infiltrated into women's mindset regarding sexual intimacy. This permissiveness has caused untold damage to the hearts, minds, bodies and identities of men and women.

Sexual intimacy outside the covenant of marriage is only one way we do a disservice to God and ourselves regarding our bodies. There are many more ways we damage our bodies: drugs, excessive alcohol, a lazy or extreme lifestyle, and even lack of rest. God tells us to work six days and rest on the seventh.

Our bodies are meant to be cared for and treated with respect. They are not to be abused or worshipped. Our bodies belong to the Lord, and they are the temple of the Holy Spirit. They no longer belong to us.

New Creation, New Spirit. Ezekiel 36:27: *"I will put My Spirit within you and cause you to walk in my statutes, and you will keep My judgements and do them."* The Spirit of the Lord residing in us empowers us to walk in the ways of God. His Spirit within us helps us to keep the judgements (commandments) of God. The New Spirit dwelling within us provides the strength and encouragement we need to live out the statutes of God.

This is the life we have chosen to live when we choose Jesus Christ as our Lord and Savior. It's a life lived in pursuit of obeying and living the commands of God. We struggle so much with this Truth because we fail to realize that in obedience to the commands of God, we find greater freedom than we could ever hope or imagine. We think we're giving up our "rights", and somehow that diminishes who we are. Giving up these "rights" does not diminish us; instead it is in giving them up that we are set free to become all we were meant, by God, to become.

"For I know the thoughts that I think toward you, says the LORD, thoughts of peace and not of evil, to give you a future and a hope" (Jeremiah 29:11). The heart God had when Jeremiah penned these words is the same heart He has for us today. His heart is for us to experience peace, to have a future and a hope. But those can only be found by pursing His way, not ours, and certainly not the world's ever-shifting culture.

His Spirit within us will never come into agreement with anything other than His commands, Will, Truth and heart. Therein lies the struggle. Whenever His Spirit confronts anything we are thinking, feeling or doing that is against God's statutes and judgements, it is uncomfortable. It causes a struggle between our will and God's Will. We can either yield our will and trust God's as the better way—or we can ignore God's commands, and pursue the course of action we wanted. God gives us the choice, and with that choice, He will also allow us to go through the resulting consequences. Those consequences are often painful and hopefully make such an impression that we never want to endure them again.

One of His commands is: *"You shall not covet your neighbor's house, you shall not covet your neighbor's wife, nor his male servant, nor his female servant, nor his ox, nor his donkey, nor anything that is your neighbor's"* (Exodus 20:17).

Covet: *to desire inordinately (excessively); to desire that which it is unlawful to obtain or possess; in a bad sense.*

It's easy to understand why God commands against coveting someone else's wife or husband. That one is covered twice—no coveting and do not commit adultery. But what's so bad about seeing something your neighbor has and wanting it? After all, God says He wants His people to be blessed. So what's the big deal? It doesn't hurt anyone.

Wrong—it hurts you and puts you in bondage.

The New Spirit within you will nudge you when your thoughts move from "Oh, my neighbor got a new car" to "I want a new car like my neighbor has." If you don't listen to the Spirit and take that thought captive before it takes root in your heart, here are some consequences of coveting.

- Jealousy, which often leads to hatred
- Resentment, which can cause division and strife
- Discontentment, which robs you of your joy and peace
- Bitterness, which usually leads to a victim or entitlement attitude
- Pride, which ALWAYS leads to some type of downfall

I believe the biggest reason God commands us against coveting is because it creates an ungratefulness for what we do have. It robs us of dwelling in a place of peace, joy and contentment. The second is because it opens the door for other, even more destructive sins. Coveting can open the door to justifying adultery, stealing, lying, and even murder. People have killed because they wanted something that wasn't theirs. The path that led to murder started with a thought, then turned into coveting, which gave birth to lust and ended in death.

Social media has opened such a powerful door to covetousness. It can steal, kill and destroy you if you do not listen to the Holy Spirit and take thoughts captive.

God has given us a New Spirit that resides within us to walk out the commands of God. This isn't to control us like puppets, but to set and keep us free from the bondage and destruction of sin. The Spirit within us teaches us the ways of God so that it will go well with us all the days of our lives. We have been made into a new creation, guided by the Spirit within us.

You have a new nature. 2 Peter 1:4 teaches us, *"...by which have been given to us exceedingly great and precious promises, that through these you may be partakers of the divine nature, having escaped the corruption that is in the world through lust."*

As a new creation, we are partakers of the divine nature of Jesus Christ. The old nature, the one that causes us to do things we shouldn't do, has been put to death. Yes, we still must work through the process. But receiving a new nature enables us to overcome from a place of victory instead of defeat.

Our old nature's first instinct is to hide, to preserve and protect self. Most times, when you ask a toddler if they ate a cookie without permission, their answer is an emphatic no. It doesn't matter if they have cookie crumbs on their face—they will deny it with every fiber of their being. They didn't learn to deny; it came naturally. They must be taught to tell the truth, but lying comes pretty easy. That is our old nature.

A new nature comes with the joy that our sins have been pardoned. We no longer operate under its bondage, or weight. We are a new creation in Christ Jesus. We have been made right with God. He has made us right with Him. We no longer need to fear the justice of God. We live under grace. But we still must live by His commands to live in the abundant and eternal life He has provided us.

Our new nature will compel us to pursue a life worthy of the goodness of God. Our new nature no longer hungers after the things of the world, but hungers after a relationship with God, with a heart set on pleasing Him and doing the things He calls us to do.

Our new nature finds no delight in sin, so the Spirit within us guides us to avoid sin. As this process matures in us, sin no longer has dominion over us. We are a new creation, made free through the renewing of our minds and partakers of Christ's divine nature.

Knowing we are a new creation with a new nature gives a higher perspective and a deeper understanding to Matthew 5:6: *"Blessed are those who hunger and thirst for righteousness, for they shall be filled."*

The more our old nature is put to death, and our new nature takes up residence, a hunger and thirst is created in us for more of God and His ways. We begin to see the futility of the world and comprehend the eternal truth and life of His. We hunger and thirst for righteousness, to be right with God, to live right, to think right, to behave according to the eternal and unshakable Truth of God's commands. We shall be filled.

Filled: *to fill or be satisfied.* What a way to live!

Dealing with Legalism

Legalism: *strict, literal, or excessive conformity to the law or to a religious or moral code* (Merriam-Webster Dictionary).

There are absolutes in God's commands we are all to live our lives by. They are summed up by Jesus in this manner: *"Jesus said to him,*

"'You shall love the Lord your God with all your heart, with all your soul, and with all your mind." This is the first and great commandment. And the second is like it: "You shall love your neighbor as yourself." On these two commandments hang all the Law and the Prophets'" (Matthew 22:36-40).

These two commandments embody the Law (Old Testament), and the words of the Prophets. We are to live our lives in pursuit of loving God and loving others. Here is the tension: we are to love by God's standard, not ours. He teaches us how to live, to love, by His standard.

Unfortunately, we, as imperfect humans, project our standards upon ourselves and others. We can project the revelation God has given us for our lives onto others and demand that *they* live how God has told *us* to live. We can even hold others to a different standard than we hold ourselves to. These are forms of legalism.

This is how I attempt to sum up legalism: trying to live *for* God without living *with* God. It's following His commands without pursing a relationship with Him.

It's all about relationship with God first, then others. But we can make that relationship so difficult by interjecting our requirements onto ourselves — even those God has never called us to — or by interjecting the standard God has called us to individually on to others. Each of our journeys are our own, but we are meant to do it together. The Bible is clear about accountability to one another, but it's done in love, not judgement.

Many have been taught that anger is a sin. They can become discouraged in pursing the Lord because they deal with anger. But I find no verse in the Word of God that says anger is a sin. There are verses about dealing with anger, hanging out with angry people, and being an angry person. We are called to put away anger, meaning not to live in an angry state, but becoming angry is not a sin. Anger, though, can *lead* to sin when not controlled. Self-control is a fruit, a by-product of listening to the Holy Spirit.

*"But I say to you that whoever is angry with his brother **without a cause** shall be in danger of the judgement..."* (Matthew 5:22a, emphasis added). The instruction Jesus is providing here leads me to understand that there are just causes to become angry. But if there is no just cause, I put myself into danger of judgement from God... not man. Even when there is just cause, I shouldn't hold on to it.

"'Be angry, and do not sin': do not let the sun go down on your wrath" (Ephesians 4:26). This is very wise advice, but still does not say anger is sin. When you let the sun go down on your wrath, it can put you into

bondage and lead you towards bitterness, an angry heart, even hatred.

There are common commandments we are all held accountable to as a new creation in Christ. There are also commandments the Lord holds us individually accountable to. James 4:17 says, *"Therefore, to him who knows to do good and does not do it, to him it is sin."*

This means that if the Lord has told me not to watch certain movies or television shows but I do, it is a sin to me. However, if I take what He told me to an extreme and I decide that I can't watch any movies or television, that moves into legalism. It's not what He said. He doesn't want me watching certain movies because they are unworthy of me and Him.

As you live out being a new creation in Christ Jesus, there will be times when you need to be very disciplined, very strict, as a new way of living becomes your nature. It takes time to break old habits, old ways of thinking and feeling, and replace them with the commandments of God.

It's no different from going on a diet. As soon as you say you're on a diet, the first thing you crave is sweets. You feel like you're deprived. It's the same tactic your flesh, and the enemy, uses to keep you from being transformed into who you were truly meant to be.

You are not going to be able do some things you used to be able to do. You can't put yourself into situations where you know you haven't built up the strength to get yourself out of when the Holy Spirit says this is heading in a bad direction.

You are a new creation in Christ Jesus. A life lived as a new creation comes with a new set of rules you need to govern your life by.

They are God's rules, set in place for your good. They are to make you FREE!

CHAPTER 5

Kingdom Mindset

"If then you were raised with Christ, seek those things which are above, where Christ is, sitting at the right hand of God. Set your mind on things above, not on things on the earth. For you died, and your life is hidden with Christ in God. When Christ who is our life appears, then you also will appear with Him in glory." (Colossians 3:1-4)

Have you heard the saying, *"so heavenly minded, no earthly good"*? We can become so spiritually minded that we don't relate to the world around us. Jesus was the most spiritually-minded man to walk this earth, yet He was still able to build relationships and transform lives with love and Truth.

We can also waste our lives away with the mindset of "when Jesus comes back" or "when I get to heaven". We are meant to change this world for God's glory until the last breath leaves our body.

God calls us to represent and advance His Kingdom here on earth. This proves to be a challenging endeavor for a number of reasons. One, we make it more complicated than He intended it to be. Two, we'd rather build *our* kingdom, because we don't understand that building God's Kingdom brings greater peace, purpose and fulfillment. And probably the most challenging is: we fail to embrace our "global" commission and our "personal" position.

We can waste our lives with the excuse of if this, if that, or if only, rather than coming into alignment with the purposes and plans God has for us.

A Kingdom-mindset is a mind set on things above, not on things on the earth. But it is not to wish and dream away your life. It's understanding the environment of God's Kingdom and how His Kingdom operates, and then learning how to live a Kingdom-minded life here on earth.

The disciples asked Jesus to teach them to pray. This prayer gives us insight into how to develop a Kingdom-mindset.

> *"Our Father in heaven, hallowed be Your name."*

This declares who we are praying to and that He is to be acknowledged first. The name Father in this context literally means *parent*. Its root means *nourisher, protector, upholder*. This implies that our prayers need to have an intimacy of relationship with the Father. We know Him. He knows us. The ability to address Him in such a personal way reveals a cultivated, personal relationship. Then the very next portion of the prayer declares that He is to be treated as sacred and be reverenced. I love how the intimacy of "Father" is taught first, then it is made abundantly clear: He is Almighty God. He is holy.

This next line of the prayer is the essence of having a Kingdom-mindset.

> *"Your Kingdom come, your Will be done on earth as it is in heaven."*

A Kingdom-mindset is knowing, through a continually growing relationship, the Heart and Will of the Father and advancing it here on earth.

People everywhere are searching for meaning, purpose and belonging to something bigger than themselves. Lives are wasting away because the truth hasn't been embraced that the greatest purpose, meaning and belonging has already been laid out before them. It's advancing the Kingdom of God. He has given each of us a role in accomplishing this task.

It is God's Will to have His Kingdom manifested here on earth. If it wasn't, Jesus wouldn't have taught us how to pray in such a bold manner. It also means that *His Kingdom come, His Will be done on earth as it is in heaven,* is possible. Let that truth soak in a bit.

Our global purpose, commission, in life is to fulfill the last command

Jesus Christ gave us: *"And Jesus came and spoke to them, saying, 'All authority has been given to Me in heaven and on earth. Go therefore and make disciples of all the nations, baptizing them in the name of the Father and of the Son and of the Holy Spirit, teaching them to observe all things that I have commanded you; and lo, I am with you always, even to the end of the age'"* (Matthew 28: 18-20).

This is the all-encompassing, Kingdom-minded purpose we are called to fulfill, and there is great passion, joy and fulfillment found in its pursuit. Everything in your life should point to fulfilling the global purpose as children of God. In Jesus Christ, you have all the authority you need to make disciples of those God puts in your path, to baptize them and teach them to obey the commands Jesus gave us.

Our global commission is to point people to Jesus and empower them to follow Him... not us. It's to teach them to become dependent upon Jesus... not us. It's to equip them on how to mine the Truth of the Word of God for themselves. It's to encourage them in their personal relationship with the Holy Spirit. It's to empower them to mature the gifts God has created them with.

Our Kingdom-minded global commission goes hand-in-hand with embracing and taking up our personal position. God formed us with a beautiful, fulfilling destiny. With His perfect destiny in mind, He gave us the gifts, desires, and capabilities to fulfill it. Remember, though, that He also gave us free will. We have the choice to embrace and pursue His plan, or deny and choose our own path.

1 Corinthians 12 is one of the guiding truths on how to embrace and fulfill the personal position God has given us. We will talk more about the gifts in an upcoming chapter; I want to focus on the fact that is it God who positions us. It is with that position in mind that God forms us, gives gifts and abilities in order to fulfill that position. The position may last a season, or a lifetime. It depends on how well you execute your responsibilities for the Lord and what God desires to accomplish.

God has orchestrated how a healthy Body of Christ should work, with everyone doing their part for the good of the whole. Verses 4-7: *"There are diversities of gifts, but the same Spirit. There are differences of ministries, but the same Lord. And there are diversities of activities, but it is the same God who works all in all. But the manifestation of the Spirit is given to each one for the profit of all"*.

There is a diversity of gifts, ministries and activities, but it is the same God who works all in all. This requires the people of God to know what gifts, ministries and activities they are called to do and learn to embrace and flourish in their God-given position. We need to not waste time coveting or being jealous over another's position.

I am gifted administratively—always have been. This is not arrogance; it is a simple statement of fact. It's how God gifted me, and environments I've been in have strengthened the gift. My mom said I would drive her crazy because I could look at a situation and within moments figure out the solution. Solutions come relatively easy to me. I'm not the brightest color in the box, so I know it's a gift from the Lord.

I am not gifted in other areas. I have learned not to view that as a negative, but as a source of blessing and protection in God's wisdom. The Holy Spirit and I are on a lifelong journey regarding my strengths and weaknesses. I usually use 'areas of opportunities' or 'challenges' for the word weakness. Too many people think of weaknesses as only a negative. Knowing your strengths and challenges is wise. It will help you avoid numerous situations that bring hurt, disappointment and even failure... failure, because you were not supposed to be in those situations in the first place.

Poor choices in my younger days derailed my childhood dreams of becoming a large-animal veterinarian. Since then, I've never really put my stake in the ground and said "I want to become a '_____.'" Rather than live in the past, and become bitter that I'll never become a veterinarian, my focus became: I want to serve Him. So what I do isn't overly important to me, but Who I serve, and how I represent Him, very much is. All that I do, however imperfectly, is for the Lord.

I've found that He always positions me in a place that require using the gifts He has entrusted me with and continual dependence upon Him to enlarge my capacity. Please do not misinterpret my not declaring becoming "insert a title" for not being intentional with my life. I am a very purpose-driven, goal-orientated individual. I rest in my Lord, but I don't let life just happen. I trust my Father, so the positions He allows me to step into I know are for my good and His glory. I do my best to move where He positions me. Then I do my best to fulfill those responsibilities with excellence. Not perfection—excellence.

My youngest daughter's experience is different. She has known, from a very early age, that she wanted to work in the medical field. She has not wavered from that path. She is a natural nurturer. She didn't get that gift from me; it is from the Lord. She has always been fascinated with the mind and has always been gifted at zeroing in on root causes way beyond her life experience. The Father created her with those gifts. He has positioned her in the church's Mother's Day Out program to utilize her nurturing gift. This position also gives her life experience in preparation for the future position God has for her.

No position is wasted unless you waste it by complaining or wishing it away instead of embracing all you are meant to learn and accomplish. There is always something valuable the Lord is trying to train and equip you in. Joy, purpose and contentment can be found in every position God places you in. You're there for a reason. If you forfeit the lesson found in one position, you run the risk of forfeiting the next position God may have for you. Embrace where God has you.

"But now God has set the members, each one of them, in the body just as He pleased. And if they were all one member, where would the body be?" Where would we be if we were all the Lead Pastor of our church? I hope you chuckled at the ridiculousness of that scenario. It would be total chaos.

There are times when I would love to tell my Lead Pastor how to do his job even more than I already do. But a Kingdom-mindset recognizes that it is God who sets the members, just as HE PLEASES. And if I do things that undermine my Lead Pastor's ability to fulfill his position as God leads him, *then I am in rebellion against God.*

When I stand before the Lord, and my life is laid out before us, He isn't going to ask me how well I did in telling others how I thought they should do their job. He will ask me—hold me accountable to—how well I stewarded the gifts and positions God gave me.

God has set me in a position to support the vision God has given the Lead Pastor, whom He also set. I am to embrace the position God has entrusted me with. I am to fulfill it with excellence because I serve Him above all others, including my Lead Pastor. I trust my Lead Pastor to fulfill his position and my Lead Pastor trusts me to fulfill my position. This trust removes schisms and divisions in the Body. God is glorified, and the Kingdom of God advances with one less speedbump.

The majority of positions are not highly visible ones. Those of us who are positioned in the hidden parts of the Body can wrestle deeply with being noticed and appreciated. The Kingdom-mindset grabs hold of the truth that God has given *"greater honor to that part which lacks it,"* so, while those in the position of being seen often get greater recognition from people, that recognition can be fickle. God says, *"those members of the body which seem to be weaker **are necessary"**, "those members of the body which we think to be less honorable, **on these we bestow greater honor;"*** God's honor is steadfast.

So, cultivate a Kingdom-mindset about your global and personal position. Do not let anyone rob you of the joy you find in serving in whatever position God has you in! Do not let coveting, wishing, or daydreaming rob you of the purpose and sense of accomplishment you find in fulfilling the requirements of your position.

Take up your position in the Body of Christ in the church you attend. If you're not serving in some capacity, you are not fully participating in the building up and advancement of the Body of Christ.

"I tithe—isn't that doing my part to serve?"

Nope. Tithing positions you for God to be able to open the windows of heaven over your life. Serving positions you to mature, use your gifts, build up the Body of Christ, find fulfilment, help others, share one another's burdens, and celebrate victories. Serving helps build healthy relationships and creates community, a sense of family, so we don't have to do life alone. Taking up your position in the Body of Christ joins and knits the whole Body together because each part supplies what is needed, and each part does its share.

God's heart for the Body of Christ is for safety to be found within the walls of the church family. It should be a place of healing, restoration, healthy growth, equipping and sending. Cultivating an atmosphere within the church walls where these things take place: messy, inconvenient, challenging—yes. Impossible—no! With God, all things are possible.

It is God's Will that things on earth are done as they are in heaven. It should start in you and within the church walls.

The global commission and personal position apply to everywhere you go. Yes, that includes outside the church walls. It includes wherever God positions you, at home or in the marketplace.

> *"…God anointed Jesus of Nazareth with the Holy Spirit and with power, who went about doing good and healing all who were oppressed by the devil, for God was with Him."* (Acts 10:38)

Let's talk about a Kingdom-mindset regarding *"who went about doing good"*. What is considered "doing good" needs to be defined how God defines good. If we go by human standards, what is considered good by one may not be considered good by another. A Kingdom-mindset always holds a thought, idea, perception, definition up to God's commands. Otherwise, you have confusion, double-mindedness, division, chaos, and ultimately inequality and injustice.

Contrary to what the world tries to say, and even what some churches teach, the Christian faith, in the purity and beauty of His Truth, is the most just and equality-based way of life anyone can live. (I'll let you pray that Truth through with the Holy Spirit.)

So, what is good by God's standard? Well, we know the Ten Commandments. Those help define God's standard of good. How do we "do good"? Part of this understanding of good can be found in Isaiah 61 and was fulfilled when Jesus read it at the temple.

Jesus Himself said, *"The Spirit of the Lord is upon Me, Because He has anointed Me to preach the gospel to the poor; He has sent Me to heal the brokenhearted, to proclaim liberty to the captives and recovery of sight to the blind, to set at liberty those who are oppressed; to proclaim the acceptable year of the Lord"* (Luke 4:18-19.)

Proclaim this over your life: *"The Spirit of the Lord is upon me. I am anointed to preach the gospel to the poor. I am sent to heal the brokenhearted with the love of God. I am equipped to proclaim the liberty of Christ to the captives. I am anointed to recover the sight of those who are blind. My life is a testimony that whom the Son sets free is free indeed."*

Doing good is loving God and loving people. Being Kingdom-minded is loving people with the love of God and the Truth of His Word — even when it is challenging, inconvenient and may hurt our own heart (to a degree). Doing good never encourages a victim mentality, nor does it enable a person to remain in a place of bondage. Doing good always loves people to a place of restoration, first to God, then within themselves, and then to others.

Your "doing good" may look different than my "doing good". You may be moved by compassion for the homeless, whereas I may be moved by compassion for those in the foster care system. So, the what and the how may look different, but the why is always the same — *"Your Kingdom come, Your Will be done on earth as it is in heaven."*

Disagreement Among Believers

Politics: one of the most polarizing topics of our day. There are Democrats, Independents, Libertarians, and Republicans who profess to know Jesus Christ as Lord and Savior. Before the election, followers of Christ are to pray and ask the Lord who they should vote for, not based on tradition, but according to whom the Lord instructs them to vote for. Followers of Jesus Christ should not be more loyal to a political party than they are to the Word of God. If we are, then that political party may be an idol in our lives.

Once the election is over, the Kingdom-minded duty for EVERY person who professes Jesus Christ as Lord and Savior is to pray for the leader. Period.

> *"Therefore, I exhort first of all that supplications, prayers, intercessions, and giving of thanks be made for all men, for kings and all who are in authority, that we may lead a quiet and peaceable life in all godliness and reverence."* (1 Timothy 2:1-3)

Why? Read verse 4: *"For this is good and acceptable in the sight of God our Savior."* End of discussion.

There is a story in Joshua 5 that really helped me start learning how to have a Kingdom-mindset regarding everything in my life. The story takes place before the Israelites are to begin taking possession of the land God had promised them. Starting in verse 13:

> *"Now when Joshua was near Jericho, he looked up and saw a man standing in front of him with a drawn sword in his hand. Joshua went up to him and asked, 'Are you for us or for our enemies?' 'Neither,' he replied, 'but as commander of the army of the Lord I have now come.' Then Joshua fell facedown to the ground in reverence, and asked him, 'What message does my Lord have for his servant?' The commander of the Lord's army replied, 'Take off your sandals, for the place where you are standing is holy.' And Joshua did so."* (Joshua 5:13-15 NIV)

I would have been surprised, even offended, by the man's answer to Joshua's question. Neither? How can it be neither? From my perspective, there are only two options; there are only two armies on this battlefield—you are either for us or them. And, by the way, do you not know who we are? We are God's chosen people! You know, the ones He delivered from Egypt. He even parted the Red Sea for us. How can you not be for us?

Joshua, even with all the time he had spent with the Lord, needed a new perspective on the reality of this battle. He failed to realize the degree the Lord was in this battle with him. God provided His own army to fight the unseen, while Joshua fought the seen. It's an even higher perspective on God working His heavenly plans and purposes to earth, through His people, for the good of those who follow Him.

The commander of the LORD's army knew, with all certainty, whom

He served, and it wasn't Joshua. He had a higher perspective; a Kingdom perspective. He fought for the LORD. So, if the LORD had told the commander to fight against Joshua to accomplish the LORD's purpose, He would have.

When you know who you truly serve, knowing where you stand is quite clear. It's on the Lord's side. It's operating from His perspective and in His Truths. It's trusting Him so completely that when someone asks, "Are you with me or them?" you can boldly, confidently and lovingly say, "Neither, I am for the Lord. Therefore, I want His Will to be done in your life and in theirs."

A person who has learned to have a Kingdom-mindset is not blind to how things are, but sees things as they should be. They have a Kingdom perspective regarding every person they meet and every situation they encounter.

Here is a situation we probably all find ourselves in. People will often come to me regarding a situation with another person. The conversation goes something like this:

> Them: "Tracy, I am really concerned about Brother A. I saw him the other night and he was pretty drunk. And I know he battles with alcohol."
>
> Me: "Have you talked to him about it?"
>
> Them: "Well, no. I'm friends with Brother A, and I don't know how he'll take it from me. I don't want to hurt our friendship."
>
> Me: "Okay, the Bible tells us that we are to go to our brothers and sisters, face to face, and talk with them directly about choices they are making that aren't in alignment with God's Word."
>
> Them: "I'm really not comfortable doing that. I thought by telling you, you'd take care of it."
>
> Me: "How is it my responsibility? I didn't see them. You did. So if I had a conversation with him, it would be based on hearsay. Then, what do you think I should say if he asks me how I heard about it? Should I tell him it was you? Lie? Or say they prefer not to be named? How do you think that would make him feel?"
>
> Them: "I didn't think about that."

71

Me: "I know you care about your brother, otherwise you wouldn't have come here in the first place. The Bible is clear on how we are to care for one another and hold each other accountable. If you truly love him, you'll love him enough to go to him and have a conversation. How he responds is up to him and between him and the Lord."

A Kingdom-mindset always goes to the Word of God on how to address any situation in their life. **It can be incredibly uncomfortable** holding yourself to this standard of life. But there is no other way to live if you want to live in true freedom.

There is a lyric to a current song that says "hard truth and ridiculous grace." A Kingdom-mindset pursues the hard Truth of God's commands and rests securely in His ridiculous grace. Grace, the free, unmerited love and favor of God that covers every misstep we make in pursuit of Him and His ways. *"Seek those things which are above... Set your mind on things above."* THE MESSAGE version verses 1-2 say it this way:

> *"So if you're serious about living this new resurrection life with Christ, act like it. Pursue the things over which Christ presides. Don't shuffle along, eyes to the ground, absorbed with the things right in front of you. Look up, and be alert to what is going on around Christ—that's where the action is. See things from his perspective."* (Colossians 3:1-2 THE MESSAGE)

Those with a Kingdom-mindset pursue the things Christ presides over. They are alert to what is going on around Christ and they train their minds and hearts to see things from His perspective. Learning to seek and set your mind on things above requires everything we've learned thus far and allowing it to transform your mind. It is the right way of thinking and approaching life.

Kingdom-minded people have set their minds on things above, not on dreaming their lives away. They have set their minds to transform this earth according to the Will of God. It is to live as Jesus lived, confronting, in love and Truth, anything that is not in alignment with heaven.

A person who cultivates a Kingdom-mindset has such a heavenly perspective that they are **earthly powerhouses**. They change the atmosphere when they walk into a room because they carry the Kingdom of God within them. They change the world in the sphere of influence God has given them because they know the Lord their God is with them. They know they hold the victory because the Lord their

God fights the battle with them.

Embrace the global commission and personal position the Lord your God has created you for. Allow the passion the Lord has placed inside you to arise and start going around and doing good in your sphere of influence. Approach every person and every situation with the Kingdom-mindset that the Spirit of the Lord is upon you and He has anointed you to bring heaven to earth.

You will encounter challenges in your pursuit of a Kingdom-mindset. The most difficult challenge will be yourself. There are some really tough situations and interesting people you'll face. You need to take a breath and live it out how God wants you to. It can be hard when someone has wounded you deeply and the Lord instructs you to hold your tongue and trust Him to work it out.

But the beauty of a Kingdom-mindset is the peace you abide in, knowing He is working ALL things out to your good and His glory.

CHAPTER 6

Yoke of Bondage

"Stand fast therefore in the liberty by which Christ has made us free, and do not be entangled again with a yoke of bondage."
(Galatians 5:1)

The love of God through Jesus Christ has made you free. You have been made free from the fear of death. You have been made free from living under the curse of works. You have been made free from the weight of sin. You have been made free from the yoke of bondage that religious works can create.

The curse of works is rooted in the original rebellion of man and revealed in the adherence to the Law to maintain right living before God. Which is impossible—outside of a belief, confession and relationship with Jesus Christ.

The Letter to the Galatians deals directly with the legalism entrenched in the minds of and demanded by the teachers of the Law in the behavior of people who were desperately trying to live pleasingly to God. They were being taught: "If you work hard enough, if you keep this law, if you give more, if you sacrifice more, if you pray more, if you do this, if you do that…, then God will love you and you will live in the blessings of God." It was a means of manipulation and control, and also a source of pride. This teaching, this mindset, this works-based way of life, is a yoke of bondage and a lie. You cannot work, nor buy, your way into God's saving grace or His blessing.

Trying to live by the Law, or rules determined by man, does not justify us; only the Blood of Jesus Christ and the grace of God does.

> *"For by grace you have been saved through faith, and that not of yourselves; it is the gift of God, not of works, lest anyone should boast. For we are His workmanship, created in Christ Jesus for good works, which God prepared beforehand that we should walk in them."* (Ephesians 2:8-10)

Our freedom from the curse of works is a gift of God, obtained only through our faith in Christ Jesus. As Ephesians 2:8-10 clearly teaches, this loving, brilliant Truth sets us free from the impossible weight of working our way to earning God's grace.

It places the responsibility of our relationship with God squarely upon our individual shoulders. It removes the legalism and laziness of trying to be in God's saving grace because of who your parents are, what's in your bank account, even what you accomplish here on earth, no matter how small or great. Your good deeds, including sharing the Gospel of Jesus Christ, will not earn God's grace. It is faith in the work Jesus Christ did through the Cross. It is your personal, ever-deepening relationship with the Father, Son, and Holy Spirit, driven deeper by your faith.

The yoke of legalism has been broken. If we allow the yoke of works to drive our relationship with the Lord, then the bondage is unworthiness, weariness and failure.

God's Word puts it this way: *"You who attempt to be justified by Law; you have fallen from grace."*

But when we understand that the gift of God broke the yoke of justification through works, then through faith, we still pursue God's standards, but we find rest in the truth that we have been saved by grace.

Legalism, saved by works, is still occurring today. We are taught in the world that if you work hard enough, you will have success. This mindset gets carried into people's relationship with God. We think if we do all the right things, strictly adhere to all the rules and regulations, we'll be right with God. It's simply not the truth. Nothing, other than confessing and our faith (belief) in Jesus Christ, saves us.

In Exodus 20:8-11, God set apart the seventh day as holy and a day of rest. It's a direct commandment of His. Legalism crept in because the Law overrode the spirit (heart) of the commandment. By Jesus' day, people took 'no work should be done' to an extreme, such as not even gathering wood for a meal. That is legalism. Jesus addressed the hypocrisy of the rules and regulations being applied to others, but not being followed themselves. He also addressed the absurdity leaders imposed by asking them if they would save one of their animals from danger on the Sabbath, which would technically be work.

Legalism says that the Sabbath is Saturday, and only Saturday. Many of us follow Sunday as the Sabbath. The **Spirit of the Law** says work six days, then set one day apart for God and rest. A Sabbath is a testimony to the world of the faithfulness and goodness of God to bless the productivity of the other six days. The command of a Sabbath is still in effect to this day. I work on Sundays, so it's not my Sabbath. I set apart another day for my day of rest.

Legalism can also creep into our lives through other avenues. These are some of the thoughts that may reveal legalism trying to get a foothold in your heart:

- I gave a lot of money, therefore that gives me a level of privilege others don't have.
- I pray x hours a day, therefore I deserve to receive favor from God.
- I served in every event the church had, so God will have to bless me.
- I helped a person in need, so I earned the right to be recognized.
- I go to this church, so I must be righteous.
- I'm a good person, therefore I am saved.

Any thought that starts with "I did" and ends with "therefore, I deserve/ earned" reveals a lack of understanding of God's gift of grace. It indicates an area of woundedness that still needs to be healed, or a lack of confidence in your identity as a child of the Most High God.

Legalism is the heart issue that says "if I work to be a better person, then God will love me." The "made us free" heart says "God loves me, so therefore I want to work at becoming the person He created me to be." Did you catch the small, but profoundly liberating, change of perspective?

The Law revealed to us that we will never achieve God's standard of living, no matter how hard we work to live out the Ten Commandments — increased to 613 commandments in Jewish Law. The "saved by grace" mindset motivates us to pursue a sinless life out of love for Him, but knowing we will be covered by grace when we miss the mark.

Do not let your guard down regarding legalism. It can worm its way into your heart, and before you know it, you are under its yoke. You'll recognize it as soon as you have the thought that you've earned or deserve something from God. God gives and He rewards, but it is on His terms, not ours. Envy can also be an indication that legalism is trying to get hold of your heart. Don't let it take root. Immediately take the thought captive, repent, replace the thought with gratitude for what work God has given you and where He has positioned you. Grace!

I heard an interesting analogy about the reality of legalism. It went something like this. A man was a drug addict. He used drugs to avoid the pain in his life. Drugs led him down a destructive path because he had to increase the frequency and intensity of the drugs to keep covering up the root of the pain. He hit rock bottom with an overdose. He survived the overdose and was invited to church. God touched His heart, and he accepted Jesus Christ as Lord. He was baptized, started attending small groups, and served in areas of the church. Everyone gave him accolades for turning his life around, and he became the church's praise report. He quit being dependent upon drugs... and became **dependent** upon the "work" of becoming a good Christian.

He worked all the Scripturally correct things, and his life was on a healthier path. But all he did was trade one addiction for another: legalism. He worked the letter of the Law (God's commands), but He never truly let Christ get to the root of the pain and bring true healing: the Spirit of the Law (relationship). So, when his past was brought into his present, all the serving in the world hadn't prepared him for it and the dependency upon drugs came back with a vengeance.

Only relationship with Jesus Christ and standing on the truth of God's Word can sustain us through the difficulties of life.

God's commands will always produce life-giving results because God set in motion the covenant of reaping and sowing. But—this is going to sound odd—His commands will only produce so much if our heart isn't transformed through abiding in relationship with Him, through Christ Jesus.

Legalism, the yoke of bondage, puts work above relationship. Liberty puts relationship above work. When liberty in Christ is first, then relationship drives the desire to do the work God has called us to, internally and externally. Then, and only then, will work not be burdensome.

Christ has made us free to live the life God intended for us. Therefore, if you truly believe in Jesus Christ as Lord and Savior, you will not use the liberty He died to give you to continue living in the bondage of legalism or sin.

We've addressed the yoke of legalism. Now let's address the yoke of sin. Remember, Jesus took care of the penalty of sin at the Cross. But we still must deal with sin in our lives, and in this world.

Sin is a yoke of bondage God never wanted for His children. He continually reveals the destructive nature of sin. He also reveals that when we are restored to Him and turn from sin, we can abide in the peace, joy and blessings He desires for us. Even when evil is present, with the chaos it brings, peace can reign.

Scripture is very clear that God has given us the ability to refuse to sin. This ability is evident in the Old Testament, long before the New Covenant of grace through Jesus Christ. And if sin, because of grace, is okay under the New Covenant, why is sin still addressed in the New Testament?

Because sin still destroys lives.

> *"So the Lord said to Cain, "Why are you angry? And why has your countenance fallen? If you do well, will you not be accepted? And if you do not do well, sin lies at the door.* ***And its desire is for you, but you should rule over it."*** (Genesis 4:6-7, emphasis added, Old Testament)

> *"No temptation has overtaken you except such as is common to man; but God is faithful, who will not allow you to be tempted beyond what you are able,* ***but with the temptation will also make the way of escape,*** *that you may be able to bear it."* (1 Corinthians 10:13, emphasis added, New Testament)

> *"I call heaven and earth as witnesses today against you, that I have set before you life and death, blessing and cursing;* ***therefore choose life,*** *that both you and your descendants may live…"* (Deuteronomy 30:19, emphasis added, Old Testament)

> *"Therefore, to him* ***who knows to do good*** *and does not do it,* ***to him it is sin.****"* (James 4:14, emphasis added, New Testament)

These Scriptures clearly reveal that we have responsibility regarding sin, and we have been given the ability to reject sin. Here comes some hard truth: the devil can't make you do anything. "I just couldn't help myself" is no excuse for allowing sin in your life. You were created with the ability to think, reason and decide for yourself. You also have the Holy Spirit guiding you to Truth.

God gave you the free will to choose, and He will allow you to choose sin.

Always remember, contained within any sin is the seed designed to destroy you. So think carefully about the choices you make and the impact they have on you and others. God, in His love for you, is relentless in pointing you away from sin and showing you the abundant life found in choosing His ways. But He will not take away your responsibility to decide for yourself.

There are many areas of sin God must deal with in our lives. Some areas we are aware of; others we may not be because we're used to them or we may be blind to them. As we walk through some of these areas, do not think that God will deal with them in the order presented. God can deal with multiple areas of our lives at the same time, or, in His wisdom, may only deal with one thing at a time. He does this because He knows us better than we know ourselves. He knows what needs to be done better than we do. So,trust His process and the order He loves you through.

An entire chapter, even a book, could be written to walk you through each of these areas. There will be enough information provided to make you aware if these are operating in your life. Trust the Holy Spirit if He urges you to pause, read, pray, study, and pray more, or gives you the thought to get more spiritual guidance in an area.

Generational Sins and Iniquity

Generational is defined as the succession of a family line. God created the family unit to be a place of safety, of healthy spiritual growth where His blessings flow. He meant fathers and mothers to pass on His Truths and goodness to their children, so His glory is revealed generation to generation. This is one of the reasons that genealogies were so important in the Word of God. They are a reminder of our heritage and the faithfulness of God.

Our childhood environment forms the foundation of how we process life. The family unit is one of the most powerfully shaping forces in our lives. We begin to model what we see in our family unit. We take on the thoughts, philosophies, vocation, church denomination, political affiliation, etc., of our family, because it's what we are exposed to by those who have the most influence over us in our formative years.

Our personalities and behavior are influenced by what we are exposed to and what we see lived out in those closest to us. We respond how we see others respond. We learn what makes those around us angry, sad, happy, excited, violent, abusive, or generous, and we adapt our responses to what we see and experience.

Then, as we grow and become exposed to more information, we have the responsibility to decide for ourselves who we are and what we believe and do. Some of those childhood teachings are healthy and grounded in truth, so hopefully we continue to mature in them and adhere to them as we move through life. Some unfortunately are not healthy, nor grounded in truth, and regrettably some are flat-out wrong, rooted in lies and pain.

For the ones God never meant to be a part of our lives, He must take us through deliverance (not an ugly word, nor a scary process), healing and a restoration process. He takes out the pain, wounds, and lies and replaces them with peace, kindness, and truth.

Some childhood influences are readily healed; others, because of the depth of impression, are more difficult and take more time. They are addressed layer by layer and replaced by precept of God by precept of God.

The following is an elementary example of how influences from childhood carry into adulthood. I started driving at a young age. I was taught the following sequence of events when backing up your car: look in the rear-view mirror, check both side mirrors, then place your right arm across the back of the seat to look over your right shoulder and reverse slowly.

I still do it today… even though my car has a back-up camera. I don't look at the image when I'm backing up. I automatically follow the process I grew up with. I don't think twice about it when I need to reverse; it's muscle memory. I'm comfortable with it and I trust it.

I had to take a little bit of time to really process this analogy given to me by the Holy Spirit. I understood the muscle memory, being comfortable, familiar with the process. Then, when the thought came up that I trusted it, the Holy Spirit made me pause to process a little deeper.

I trust the way I was trained as a child on how to reverse my car. This means I don't trust the new way of driving in reverse. It's something new. I'm familiar with the old way. Continuing in the old way doesn't require me to change, therefore doesn't require effort. I can keep doing things the exact same way I always have. I'm comfortable with what I know, even if there is a new, potentially better way to go about it.

Now, apply this to generational sins and iniquity, which are engrained in us much more deeply because of their nature. They are also more deeply engrained in us because of the degree of trauma encountered or the degree of our response to the trauma for self-preservation.

Generational Sins are not just about sinful behavior: they are when our hearts are attached to the wrong things. They are tendencies and weaknesses passed down from generation to generation.

Generational Iniquity, from *'iwwah, awon,* meaning *to bend, make crooked,* expresses *a deviation from the right path.* An iniquity is deeply rooted in us, often formed at such a young age that we're not even aware of it. A generational iniquity bends us towards an incorrect, twisted, stubborn attitude towards self, someone, a people, even God. Generational iniquity may include divorce, abuse, sexual sins, sexual perversions and addictions, other types of addictions, rage, prejudice, mental illness, sickness, laziness, poverty, involvement in false religions, criticism, resentment, shame, guilt, passivity, perfectionism, and other destructive behaviors and cycles.

We can take on hatred, prejudices, racism, bitterness, offense, and even a poverty, victim, or entitlement mentality without even realizing it. We respond or behave in ways we don't understand. Do you do things that make you wonder why? Do you respond to situations and think, "Where did that come from?" Those are possibly rooted in Generational Iniquities.

The Good News is that Jesus Christ broke the yoke of generational sins and iniquity at the Cross—so you are now responsible to God for your sins, regardless of where they originated from. Just because you grew up in an angry, abusive or addictive home, you cannot use that as a justification to remain angry, abusive or an addict.

If you have done the work to deal with personal sin, yet are still struggling with ungodly thoughts or behaviors, it could be generational sin or iniquity. You have been given the power and authority in Christ Jesus to break generational bondage from yourself and your family line.

> **Expose the sin.** The Holy Spirit will lead you to bring the iniquity into the light of God's glory. Recognize it in yourself and in your family line. It's not about digging deeply into the pain; it's about recognizing the reality of it and holding it up to God's truth and His glory.

> **Forgive.** Forgive those who have caused generational sin and

iniquity into yours and their family lineage. Remember, this is not about justice for wrongs done. Let God deal with justice. This is about setting you free. Then it's about setting your family free. This is about stopping the predisposition to wrong things and the damage it does to lives.

Repent. We don't always understand what it means to repent. Repent is defined as feeling pain, sorrow, or regret for something done or spoken. It's a grief that we, or others, have grieved the heart of God, and we make a conscious choice not to repeat the behavior.

Speak Truth. Declare that it stops with you! Hebrews 12:27 tells us that those things that can be shaken will be removed. But those that cannot be shaken, they will remain. God's Truth cannot be shaken! It will accomplish what God intends for it to accomplish.

The evidence, the manifestation, of deliverance (being set free) from generational sin or iniquity may be immediate, or it may come in stages. It depends upon how God walks you through it, or the depths of it in your being. Trust His truth and His care of you. Always know this: you are immediately set free from it. The generational sin or iniquity no longer has dominion over you. You, through Jesus Christ, have dominion over it.

Soul Ties

God created us for relationship. First with Him, then with others. Relationships were designed to enrich our lives. Because of wounds and brokenness, relationships have become unhealthy, and unfortunately destructive.

Soul ties are formed when we bond and attach ourselves to someone or something. There are healthy soul ties designed by God. Then there are unhealthy ones, created by us and the enemy.

God created the most powerful soul tie through the covenant of marriage. In Genesis 2:18, He states it is not good for man to be alone, so He made a helper comparable to man: woman. God didn't create a subservient companion. He created a helper, a helpmate, because it's not good for man, nor woman, to do life alone. Through the bond of marriage, two lives become one life. *"Therefore a man shall leave his father and mother and be joined to his wife, and they shall become one flesh."*

Jesus restated this bond in Mark 10:5-9: *"And Jesus answered and said to them, 'Because of the hardness of your heart he wrote you this precept. But from the beginning of the creation, God "made them male and female." "For this reason a man shall leave his father and mother and be joined to his wife, and the two shall become one flesh"; so then they are no longer two, but one flesh. Therefore what God has joined together, let not man separate.'"*

The soul tie in marriage is mental, physical, emotional and spiritual. It is meant to be intimacy at its most beautiful. This bond brings the strengths and weaknesses of each person to mutually benefit each other. It's the desire to serve one another and know that when they are in agreement, much more can be accomplished.

There are other examples of healthy soul ties in the Bible: Mary and Elizabeth (Luke 1), Naomi and Ruth (Book of Ruth), David and Jonathan (1 Samuel 18-20).

In not one of these examples of healthy soul ties did one relinquish their personal relationship with God, personal identity, or individual purpose or calling. They mutually served and encouraged one another. They respected, honored and loved each other. They validated each other's worth. And they had healthy, God-instructed boundaries. There is an intimacy and trust in each of these examples, but nothing compared to the intimacy of the marriage covenant God designed.

When we step out of healthy soul ties and enter unhealthy ones, we become fractured. We lose a piece of ourselves. We relinquish pieces of our souls to others or other things. Our souls belong to the Lord and when any of it has been given to anyone or anything else, there is a void. We are not whole.

Unhealthy, ungodly soul ties are formed when we operate out of God's mandates and relationships are built on lies and deceptions. When our identity and validation is not based on God's Truth and love, we have no true sense of self. No sense of our God-given identity can cause us to seek out validation wherever we can find it, and we are willing to become like everybody else to fill the void.

We develop emotional and even sexual soul ties with wounded and broken people, in the desire to be validated and loved. This may give an initial season of happiness, but it will always lead to dissatisfaction, and often mutual destruction.

The identity and sexuality of men (masculinity) need to be affirmed and respected as God intended. God validated Jesus Christ's identity and His love for Him when He said, *"This is my Son, in whom I am well pleased."* The identity and sexuality of women (femininity) need to be acknowledged and honored as God intended. God validated women's worth throughout the Old Testament. Jesus confirmed women's worth throughout His time on earth.

God created male and female. Masculinity and femininity are a created thing. Our sexual identities are not our all-encompassing identities, and they are not to be worshipped. When God-created sexuality is distorted through lies or trauma, confusion enters our perception of God and self.

If men's and women's God-given identity and sexuality are not affirmed by 'authority' figures in their lives (parents, pastors, godly friends, even bosses), then they will seek out affirmation wherever they can find it… promiscuousness, pornography, materialism, even a willingness to engage in acts of degradation. We will seek out a cheap substitute, all in the desire to love and be loved.

Soul ties can also manifest in objects and living our lives through the lives of others (social media), or our children. Social media superficially feeds our desire for connection and relationship, but it is false, a lie, as it requires no intimacy, authenticity or work.

John 4 tells a beautiful story of how Jesus broke unhealthy soul ties for a woman and restored her to her true identity and the beauty of her femininity. In summary, Jesus met a Samaritan woman at a water well. For Jesus to speak to a woman, much less a Samaritan woman, was radical! He broke significant cultural and traditions of the day. He told her there was a better way to fill the brokenness in her heart. Then He spoke directly to how she was filling the void, and it was without judgement. He opened the door for her to choose if she wanted to stay in her current circumstance, or not settle for second best. She kept questioning Jesus. Jesus kept answering. Then she ran and told those in the city about the man she had met. She chose to be changed.

All it took for the yoke of soul ties to be broken from her life was pure, no-strings-attached love, and being told the truth. She needed to hear that she was more than what her past said she was, and that she deserved to be treasured by a husband.

You too can stand in the liberty Christ has given you by breaking off unhealthy soul ties. Ask God to reveal Himself to you as your Father. Renounce, in the name of Jesus Christ, any unhealthy soul tie in your life and take back the entirety of your soul, committing it to the lordship of Jesus Christ. Ask the Holy Spirit to refresh your mind and emotions and restore all that unhealthy soul ties have stolen.

Do not become entangled with the yoke of unhealthy soul ties again. You are worth more than they provide.

The Flesh

Our own flesh is one of the biggest challenges we need to overcome in order to live in the liberty of Christ. The flesh can be defined as our own personal and selfish desires/wants that are contrary to the commands of God. It's also about bringing into submission those things that may not technically violate the Word of God, but still bring you into bondage.

Paul says it like this in 1 Corinthians 6:12: *"Just because something is technically legal doesn't mean that it's spiritually appropriate. If I went around doing whatever I thought I could get by with, I'd be a slave to my whims"* (THE MESSAGE).

God understands the challenges we have with our selfish desires, but that does not mean He tolerates them in our lives. In His grace, He always provides a way to get out of them (1 Corinthians 10:13).

The sin of the flesh always starts with the eyes. We see something and we want it (coveting). If we don't take that thought captive, desire enters in and takes over. The Bible is very blunt about ungodly desire and its ensuing consequences.

> *Then, when desire has conceived, it gives birth to sin; and sin, when it is full-grown, brings forth death.* (James 1:15)

Consequences are clear... sin brings forth death. Period.

The motivation to choose or not to choose to sin is driven by your relationship with the Father and the Son. The closer you draw to Him, the more you won't want to sin. You can, through Jesus Christ, learn to bring to an end, crucify, the desires of the flesh.

> *"And those who are Christ's have crucified the flesh with its passions and desires."* (Galatians 5:24)

This doesn't mean thoughts won't pop up—but if you are Christ's you learn how to quickly deal with it, so it doesn't produce death in your life.

Your relationship with Christ should compel you **to pursue a sinless**

life. The Father and Christ's love for you and your ever-deepening love for the Father and Christ creates in you a heart that doesn't want to sin against Him.

> *"We know that whoever is born of God does not sin; but he who has been born of God keeps himself, and the wicked one does not touch him."* (1 John 5:18)

Your relationship with the Father protects you from the enemy. What a powerful and liberating promise!

Christ has made us free from the yokes of legalism, generational sin and iniquity, soul ties, and the flesh. Do not be entangled with them anymore.

The Right Kind of Work

There is a type of work we should all be pursuing. This type of work is a good work, where His grace is sufficient for you to be able to accomplish all things in Him.

Ephesians 2:8-10 says *"good works, which God prepared beforehand that we should walk in them."*

God created man(kind) to work, to produce, be fruitful. He never meant for us to be idle. Even in the Garden of Eden, a place of perfection, God prepared a good work for us to walk in.

> *"God took the Man and set him down in the Garden of Eden to work the ground and keep it in order."* (Genesis 2:15, THE MESSAGE)

God has invited us, through Jesus Christ, to be a part of the good work He has been doing since time began. We join Him in His work; He tends not to join us in our self-promoting work.

There are several elements to keep pursuing regarding the good works we are to walk in. Preparation is imperative. God needs to make us ready for the good works He has prepared for us. Moses spent forty years in the desert preparing for God's good work of leading the Israelites out of the bondage of Egypt. Joseph spent time in slavery, then in prison in preparation for becoming the second most powerful man in Egypt. Jesus spent 30 years in relative seclusion before the time was right to begin the work God had Him to do.

We are God's workmanship; we are to reflect His goodness and faithfulness in our lives. It's who we were meant to be, and it gives us the greatest peace, joy and fulfillment. Because God knows this, He is relentless to produce Christ in us. He wants our minds to be renewed to think like Jesus (2 Corinthians 4:16, Ephesians 4:20-24, Colossians 3:10). He wants our hearts to love as Christ loves (1 John 3:16, 1 Timothy 1:5, 2 Timothy 2:22, 1 Peter 1:22).

And we are purposed to work as Jesus worked. We are to be about our Father's business (Luke 2:49).

But work is always relationship first, purpose second.

We are designed to produce, to bear fruit. It is an essential element to our divine make-up. When we are not producing, we are withering. Producing fruit brings life, and continued faithfulness brings more life.

> *"I am the true vine, and My Father is the vinedresser. Every branch in Me that does not bear fruit He takes away; and every branch that bears fruit He prunes, **that it may bear more fruit**."* (John 15:1-2, emphasis added)

Working for the Lord and bearing fruit doesn't stop as we age.

> *"They shall still bear fruit in old age; They shall be fresh and flourishing."* (Psalm 92:14)

It is not necessarily about what work you do; it is more essential to know Who you are doing it for and why you are doing it.

> *"And whatever you do, do it heartily, as to the Lord and not to men, knowing that from the Lord you will receive the reward of the inheritance; for you serve the Lord Christ."* (Colossians 3:23-24)

Are you working for the Lord?

CHAPTER 7

Lies We Believe

"And the Lord God said to the woman, 'What is this you have done?'
The woman said, 'The serpent deceived me, and I ate.'"
(Genesis 3:13)

The story of the interaction between Eve and the serpent is a pattern of deception we still encounter today. God tells us something and instead of trusting and standing on His Truth, we allow other voices, including our own reasoning, to distort or deny His Truth. We believe a lie over Truth.

There are so many lessons in the first three chapters of Genesis to be learned. The lesson I want to take from this is how easy it is for Truth to be manipulated, distorted, or taken out of context (a subtler form of manipulation), and for destruction to enter our lives. It is heartbreaking, and a little scary, how easily out-and-out lies can enter our lives and we begin to operate our lives based on lies, rather than Truth.

Eve usually gets most of the blame, but Adam was just as culpable in this interaction. Both believed the distortion/manipulation rather than listening to God's instructions and believing in the consequences God said would follow. God's Word is filled with the reality of consequences. He repeatedly warns of destructive consequences that will occur if His Word is not heeded.

The lie the serpent told them opened the door to distorting the proper alignment of relationship and knowledge. Adam and Eve chose to put knowledge above relationship. Knowledge processed through relationship with God and His Truth brings greatness. Knowledge processed through man's lens and limitations brings confusion, chaos and, ultimately, destruction.

This misalignment of relationship and knowledge continues to plague us. God must be first, and knowledge must be filtered through His Truth. God is not intimidated nor fearful of man having knowledge. In fact, God gives knowledge to man. He gives us gifts of knowledge and of understanding. He empowered and equipped us to think, reason and to understand.

But when we take Him out of the equation, the essential keystone to true knowledge is removed. It limits us from knowing who He is and who we truly are.

Lies can take root in us through various avenues. Once a lie takes root, it begins to distort reality and we begin to process life through distorted knowledge. Understanding of God, self, and others then becomes distorted because the knowledge we received was faulty.

Once we begin to operate out of this place of distortion, wrong thinking, it becomes a stronghold in our lives. God must break down those strongholds, so knowledge and understanding is restored and processed through relationship.

Relationship is with the Source, not the knowledge. When knowledge is first, it is an idol.

Strongholds are established through a sequence of events. An incident occurs; it's usually a negative or unhealthy event, but not always. We then create a narrative in order to cope with the event, or to come to some type of understanding of why it occurred. The narrative is created through our personal interpretation and influenced by the words and actions of others. The next step is to determine how we are going to ease our pain or protect ourselves in the future. Our newly set up defense mechanism holds people at arm's length, creating the opportunity for a similar event to occur, and the cycle continues and is reinforced.

Strongholds can be established through good events too. Someone comes up to you and says, "You did such a great job with that project. I wish I could be that good." You say, "Thank you." A bit later the thought enters your mind: "I really *did* do a great job." But the thoughts don't end with "Thank you, Lord." You continue down the cycle, building a narrative of how well you did. You tell yourself that no one could have done it better, and you deserve to be recognized. Then someone else comes along and congratulates you again, and instead of simply saying "thank you," you proceed with telling them all about... you. This pattern of thinking will build a stronghold in your life, and the outcome of it will be pride. The consequence of pride is a downfall. Always.

We are called to be co-laborers with Christ. There is a beautiful balance with God getting all the glory and you being a gracious and humble servant of the Lord. It's found with relationship first, work (knowledge) second. Are you seeing a pattern here?

Only the Truth and love of Jesus Christ can break the cycle. Jesus must be invited in to heal the pain. He will never force healing and restoration, but He will be relentless in providing the opportunity to be made whole. People can function for years, even professing themselves a believer of Him, and never allow His love to heal them and restore accurate thinking patterns.

Father/Mother Wounds

God created the family unit to be a place of safety, where healthy identities are established, and God-given destinies are nurtured. The breakdown of the family unit has brought deeply seated wounds, insecurities and strongholds of incorrect beliefs of God, self and what life can be.

Father and mother wounds can also occur in the most loving of homes. They should not be discounted because someone else had a worse homelife. Any wound needs to be healed, and proper thoughts need to be instilled. There is no perfect parent, and it is not dishonoring when parental shortcomings are acknowledged and forgiven. There is no place for disrespect, though.

Fathers are supposed to draw out and affirm children's God-given identities. Mothers are created to be nurturers and bring security into children's sense of well-being. This brilliant integration of the strengths of both parents creates an atmosphere where children can flourish. It is also an earthly representation of a heavenly Father and creates a knowing of the need to be in right relationship with Him.

When either one of these vital roles is distorted or absent in the lives of children, the wounds formed cause children to ease the pain, or fill the void, through any readily accessible means. Far too often these means, which may ease pain and bring acceptance in the beginning, quickly disintegrate into destruction. Wounded people, especially predators, can spot hurting people and manipulate them.

Jesus Christ heals and makes us free from any stronghold created by father and mother wounds. Any wound that distorts one's perspective of God and His love for us, He will deal with—no matter how big or small the distortion in thinking may be.

We are sons and daughters of the Lord God Almighty. This is who we are, and it is foundational in discovering our true identity. He is our Father. He is our Source for all things. We process all things through Him and His Truth first.

Healing from father and mother wounds starts with you repenting from any resentment, bitterness, anger, offense, or unforgiveness you harbor towards your father or mother. Remember, this isn't necessarily about them; it's about you receiving the healing you need in your life. They may or may not be a part of this process—that's for God to determine. This is between you and Jesus, so you are made free and form empowering thinking patterns.

Do not forget the Holy Spirit in your healing process. Ask Him to bring the healing power and presence of Jesus Christ in your life and remind you not to revert to old patterns. He is your Teacher. Allow the love of God to permeate your life. He is your Father. You are His.

Rejection

We've all experienced rejection in one form or another. Rejection from family, friends, even strangers, and nowadays, social media. There is also perceived rejection because we're operating out of insecurity.

The primary root of rejection is the feeling of not being loved or accepted. The good news is that we have a Heavenly Father and Savior who promises to care for us and will never leave nor forsake us. But for us to believe this Truth, we must allow the love and acceptance found in Jesus Christ to anchor us. When we are anchored in the love and acceptance of Jesus Christ, rejection, which will happen throughout life, does not lessen our sense of worth.

Roots of rejection are often related to birth or instilled during our young, formative years. Rejection can stem from abandonment, feelings of being in the way or ignored, adoption, our parents preferring a different gender, births due to an unplanned pregnancy, or numerous other reasons. Divorce, and the dynamics of blended families, can also cause feelings of rejection.

Words we allow to take root in our thinking can create strongholds of rejection. Being told that we're stupid, not good enough, or will never belong warps our perception of who we really are.

Rejection when not healed by the acceptance of Jesus Christ can cause self-hatred, self-condemnation, and a constant desire to become whoever or do whatever is necessary to be accepted by whomever. It doesn't matter if it's harmful to us; we just want to feel like we belong somewhere. It is not love when demands are made, and performance is required to be someone you're not (and it violates who God says you are).

Rejection is a lie meant to keep you separated from the Truth. Rejection keeps you isolated. Isolation reinforces your thoughts about being rejected… creating a stronghold in your life.

The stronghold of rejection is broken by God's Truth and healed only through acceptance.

The most important acceptance you need to experience and believe is that you have been accepted by Almighty God. And you are loved just as you are… Remember, though, being loved and accepted right where you are now doesn't mean that He will allow you to stay just as you are. He will work to transform your heart and your mind to think according to His Truth.

God is the source of your identity and your destiny. It is Him and His Truth which defines you. He is the One who determines your value. Do not allow anyone else to make you feel less than who He says you are.

Ask the Lord to forgive you for allowing others and the enemy to make you feel rejected. Repent of allowing rejection to create incorrect thought patterns in your life.

Forgive those who have rejected you through words and/or actions. Ask the Holy Spirit to cease any residual consequences formed out of responding to rejection.

Replace every lie that reeks of rejection with the Truth of the Word of God. There is a Scripture in God's Word that eradicates every one of those lies. Hold fast to God's Truth until they form correct thinking patterns about rejection.

Shame

Shame is an internal narrative we tell ourselves that reinforces the lie we are not good enough. We set ourselves up as our own judge and condemn ourselves to never being able to measure up. Measure up to what? It's never clearly known—we believe we are simply less than that invisible standard.

Shame takes hold when we try and hide an action that violated a principle of God. Everyone feels shame when they first do something that is wrong. People can deny it all they want to; the truth is, we all have an internal voice that says, *"You really shouldn't do that."*

For me, it's the Holy Spirit; others may call it a conscience. I personally do not believe that the Holy Spirit and a person's conscience are the same. The Holy Spirit is directed by God and will always align with God's Truth. A conscience may have a degree of morality, but it is influenceable by emotions, culture, trends, and our personal convictions and philosophies. The Holy Spirit can transform our conscience to align with God's Truth, but the conscience will never influence the Holy Spirit.

Adam and Eve felt shame when they trusted the voice of the enemy over the instruction of the Lord. They used their limited knowledge to try and deal with their shame. First, they tried to cover themselves up. Then, when they heard God, they tried to hide from Him. Don't we do the same thing? It didn't work for them, and it doesn't work for us.

The cycle of shame is the same as any other stronghold; the difference is that we inflict shame upon ourselves. We choose to do something we know we shouldn't, and the thought comes: "Look what you've done now; what is everyone going to think about you?" Instead of owning up to it straight away, we try to cover it up with either denial or lies. Then the fear of being found out takes hold, and we are trapped. Fear helps keep shame in darkness, where shame thrives and destroys you from the inside out.

It can also take hold when we do not confront an unhealthy thought with God's Truth. A thought is not a sin until we allow it to get to our heart and it becomes desire. Our first response to an unhealthy or immoral thought is often "Oh my goodness, I'm such a horrible person for thinking that; I'll never be a good enough person," when the first response should be, "I refuse to think about that, I choose to think about things that are true, noble, just, pure, lovely, and of a good report" (Philippians 4:8)—and then move on.

Shame has become an ugly word in today's culture. There is a healthy side of shame, and it can used by the Holy Spirit to let us know we shouldn't have done what we did. The emotion of shame is an opportunity to repent, ask for forgiveness, and put the incident behind us before it takes root and becomes a stronghold.

This includes trusting God and having the courage to face things you may have done in your past. If you don't deal with your past and the shame it carries, then you are still giving it the power to hold in bondage your present and future. It takes courage to bring into the light a lie you've been living for potentially years.

I remember when I first confessed I had had an abortion. I was so afraid I would be judged, hated, rejected and all the other negative narratives I repeated to myself. But the shame of having an abortion was defining who I was, and it was destroying me and my dreams. The truth is, some people have judged and rejected me, but those who understood the grace of God stood by me and helped me live out forgiveness. I harbor no bitterness towards those who have judged or rejected me; that is between them and God. What I do know is that the confession of abortions broke shame off my life and made me free. And, most importantly, the only One who could do that has never rejected me.

Shame no longer causes me to live beneath my God-given potential and destiny. But I still carry grief. There are always consequences. Grief, as with shame, does not define me.

I can process the reality of what I chose to do. But those choices no longer hold me in bondage. I no longer believe the lies I and the enemy were telling me. Lies such as 'I will never be a mother after what I have done'. Freedom in Christ tells me I am worthy to be a mother, not just to my children, but to those who don't have a mother influence in their lives. I view my life through the eyes of how God sees me. Not man (or woman).

There is nothing arrogant or prideful about a healthy self-image. God wants us to have a true understanding of who we are. He created us to desire a sense of belonging, to abide in a sense of worth, being valued for who we are and rejoicing in the truth that we are highly capable individuals.

Breaking off the shackles of shame allows you to see yourself as God sees you. It opens your heart and expands your understanding of grace. It opens the floodgates of God's heart of mercy and grace over your life. As you learn to receive and abide in His grace, you are able to extend it to others.

Take a moment to ask the Holy Spirit to reveal the roots, the access point, of shame in your life. Confess it to the Lord, repent, and reject the root and effects shame has had in your life. Then, open your heart to receive the healing power of God's grace.

Core Lies

There is an old saying that goes like this: *"Sticks and stones may break my bones, but words will never hurt me."*

What a lie! Words hurt, and do more long-term damage than a broken bone. Words have the power to destroy destinies and bring forth death. They also have the power to heal and give life.

> *"Words kill, words give life; they're either poison or fruit—you choose."* (Proverbs 18:21, THE MESSAGE)

Core lies are created as we process the words and actions of others towards us. The closer the person is to us, the more embedded into our being the core lie becomes. The more we hear it, the more it's reinforced, and it becomes truth to us. Then core lies begin to define our identity and set limitations on our capability to achieve anything. Core lies have the ability for us to separate ourselves from God, because we can't reconcile the lie we're telling ourselves with the Truth of who He says He is. We process who God is, and His promises, based on the core lie we believe.

So, if we believe we are unlovable, then it's difficult to believe that God can love us.

If our earthly father told us we will never amount to anything, we process God through that core lie's lens. These, and other core lies, are negative "I am" statements:

- I am unwanted.
- I am worthless.
- I am better off on my own.
- I am a disappointment.
- I destroy everything I touch.
- I am a failure.
- I don't deserve to be happy.

God established the law of reaping and sowing.

> *"Do not be deceived, God is not mocked; for whatever a man sows, that he will also reap. For he who sows to his flesh will of the flesh reap corruption, but he who sows to the Spirit will of the Spirit reap everlasting life. And let us not grow weary while doing good, for in due season we shall reap if we do not lose heart."* (Galatians 6:7-9)

Sowing to the flesh means you are feeding, encouraging, giving life to the flesh. If you keep telling yourself you're not good enough, it will bring forth evidence that reinforces the lie. Some may call it a self-fulfilling prophecy.

You believe you're not good enough to have a good relationship. So, out of your desire to have companionship and be accepted, you adapt your behavior to what you think that person wants. Out of fear and insecurity, your behavior is inconsistent, causing the other person to put up walls. You sense the distancing, and either try harder to do whatever it takes to maintain a relationship with this person—which will cause the person to put up more boundaries—or you walk away from the relationship, with the core lie further reinforced.

You can't have good, healthy relationships when the parties involved are not secure in their identities and have a healthy viewpoint of themselves and their values. It's the same with God. It's difficult to have a relationship with Him when insecurities and fears keep the walls of protection up. Always know, God is secure in who He is: He isn't changing. He changes us through holding up the core lies you believe to the light of His Truth and His love.

There is a Truth in God's Word that breaks every lie. When you speak God's Truth over the lie and your life, you begin to feed the Spirit. Sow truth to the Spirit and life will come forth; identities are restored; dreams come true; joy, hope and peace are reaped.

Do you want to break core lies from your life? Look up and read the verses beside each of the lies. Write them down and ask the Holy Spirit to reveal the heart of God to you in each of these verses.

- I am unwanted (Hebrews 13:5; Matthew 18:14).
- I am worthless (John 3:16).
- I am better off on my own (Ecclesiastes 4:9-12; Proverbs 27:17).
- I am a disappointment (Psalm 139:14).
- I destroy everything I touch (Ephesians 2:10; 2 Chronicles 31:21).
- I am a failure (Psalm 138:8; Jeremiah 29:11).
- I don't deserve to be happy (John 10:10; Galatians 5:22-23).

These are only a few examples of how the Truth of God exposes and overrules core lies. The darkness of lies cannot stand up against the light of God's Truth. His truth is backed up with His power, authority, and Sovereignty. His Truth will always prevail.

As with Adam and Eve, once Truth has been revealed to us, we become accountable to what we do with it. Adam and Eve both suffered **individual** consequences as a result of their **individual** decision to not take God at His Word.

So, you can continue to choose to believe you are unwanted—or you can choose to believe that God's heart is that NOT ONE PERSON PERISH (Matthew 18:14)!

Never again allow core lies to become a stronghold in your life. Never again allow them to define who you are or determine what you are capable of accomplishing. Take words and thoughts captive and hold them up to the Truth of God. Cling to what is good, always!

Inner Vows

Inner vows are those promises we make to ourselves to create a place of self-preservation due to a painful, confusing, or traumatic event. They are often made when we are quite young, or amid trauma, and we forget we make them. But they have taken root in our mind, and subconsciously begin to form internal defense mechanisms as an attempt to keep us from pain.

However, the reality of what inner vows produce is bitterness, isolation and loneliness; if not healed by the goodness of God, they will eventually become deep-seated anger and hatred.

Inner vows most likely begin with, "I will NEVER _____." (Be hurt like this again; be like my father/mother; trust anyone.) Statements like this set yourself up as your own protector, defender, judge, and jury, and it's impossible to be that for yourself. By trying to protect yourself from the negative aspects of life, you isolate yourself from being able to embrace and enjoy the very best life and relationships have to offer.

You set your capabilities above God's abilities, therefore you set yourself up as an idol in your own life. You know better than God.

Be made free from Inner Vows.

Repent for making the vow; it doesn't necessarily matter the circumstance. God understands why you did it at the time. But now you know He is your Source; you are not your own source.

Forgive those who have hurt you. Remember, forgiveness is about setting yourself free. It doesn't mean you have to let those who have hurt you back into your life at this time. God forgave you. You don't have the right to withhold forgiveness.

Break your agreement with yourself on how to deal with hurt, pain, and wounds. Ask the Lord to become your Healer and Comforter.

Break your alignment with the enemy in dealing with pain. From this moment on, you work through your pain with Almighty God, through the power of His Holy Spirit.

Renounce any agreement that may have been handed to you generationally.

Declare that inner vows and the effects they have had are broken from your life.

Now the most important step to maintaining freedom from the lies we believe: ***DEVELOP NEW, SCRIPTURE-BASED BEHAVIORS!***

We have a very real enemy. His name is satan. I don't tend to focus on him too much, because Jesus Christ defeated him at the Cross, and the Bible gives clear instruction on how to deal with him. But it would be foolish to ignore the reality that satan wants to steal, kill, and destroy your life.

Jesus Christ told us the dangers of being set free, but not filling our being with the Truth and promises of God.

> *"When a corrupting spirit is expelled from someone, it drifts along through the desert looking for an oasis, some unsuspecting soul it can bedevil. When it doesn't find anyone, it says, 'I'll go back to my old haunt.'* ***On return, it finds the person swept and dusted, but vacant.*** *It then runs out and rounds up seven other spirits dirtier than itself and they all move in, whooping it up. That person ends up far worse than if he'd never gotten cleaned up in the first place."* (Luke 11:25-27, THE MESSAGE, emphasis added)

I am not implying you have a corrupting spirit. I am pointing out the Truth that if you don't change your habits from old ways to new, Christ's ways, you increase the likelihood of becoming worse off. And capture that thought right now trying to tell you that maybe it's better not to be healed and restored. It's a lie. The enemy always wants to keep you bound. Jesus Christ always wants to make you free.

The Lord has made me free. That doesn't mean I don't have times of hurt, disappointment, or even isolation. I'm still on this earth, so those things will occur. The difference is that instead of trying to protect and heal myself, I take it to the Lord. He and I have a wonderful, personal place we go to.

I find a quiet place. I begin to talk to the Lord about the situation and how I feel. And, yes, these conversations can be quite animated. He always patiently listens. Then I get quiet and wait. I know He is already with me, but depending on what He knows I need, He reveals Himself in some way. I can feel His presence more deeply. He gives me a mind picture (I love those). A Scripture comes to mind. Mostly, it's an overwhelming knowing that He is with me, I am loved, and it's going to be okay. He will make a way.

The above is the new behavior I follow, and it took time and practice to get into place. This new way of approaching life has become muscle memory. It broke the stronghold of ranting, raving, isolation, striking out, gossiping, or anger I used to default to when I was in pain.

God will expose any lie in your life. Seize the opportunity to no longer be deceived, and live in the freedom His Truth brings.

CHAPTER 8

Planted

"Blessed is the man who trusts in the Lord, And whose hope is the Lord. For he shall be like a tree planted by the waters, Which spreads out its roots by the river, And will not fear when heat comes; But its leaf will be green, And will not be anxious in the year of drought, Nor will cease from yielding fruit." (Jeremiah 17:7-8)

If you're anything like me, you skimmed over the verse and started reading. Lucky for us both, we're going to break these verses down, so they get deep into our being and transform us from the inside out.

These words were spoken from Almighty God to the Prophet Jeremiah, so they are Truth, unshakeable, irrevocable and eternal. They present the perpetual evidence of a person's life when they are rooted and grounded in their relationship with God.

"Blessed is the man who trusts in the Lord..."

Blessed, *made happy or prosperous, prosperous in worldly affairs; enjoying spiritual happiness and the favor or God* (Webster's 1828 dictionary).

God wants people to live a happy and prosperous life. He desires for people to enjoy contentment in every aspect of their life and abide in His favor. The biggest hindrance to living a blessed life is us. We want to define what "blessed," happiness, looks like, and we want to decide how we get it. The truth is, most of us have no idea what makes us genuinely happy.

Precious moments of our lives are stolen with the "if onlys". If only I had better parents. If only I had a better job. If only I wasn't in debt. If only I had a more supportive spouse. If only someone had given me a break. If only...

Or we rob the joy of the now moments with the "when and then" thief. When I graduate high school, then... When I have money, then... When I get married, then... When I get divorced, then... When my children graduate, then... When I get that promotion, then... When I retire, then...

The secret of a blessed life is found in trusting the Lord with your life. Trust is a confidence that no matter the circumstance, or deep the pain, the promises of God will prevail. The key to unlocking the secret of a blessed life is to take everything, good, bad, and ugly, to Him. It's about doing life with Him at the center.

"And whose hope is the Lord."

Hope, *a desire of something good, accompanied with at least a slight expectation of obtaining it, or a belief that it is obtainable; confidence in a future event; the highest degree of well-founded expectation of good* (Webster's 1828 dictionary).

Pay close attention to the 'ands' and 'buts' in the Word of God. The verse says, *"Blessed is the man who trusts in the Lord,* **AND** *whose hope is the Lord."* Trust and hope intermingle, but they cover different areas of your relationship with the Lord. Trust is a decision of the mind; hope leans more towards a decision of the spirit.

Isaiah 26:3 tells us, *"You will keep him in perfect peace, Whose mind is stayed on You, Because he trusts in You."* We make intentional decisions in our mind to trust in Him. We've discussed how we need to replace old ways of thinking, core lies, etc., with the truth of God's promises. Why? Because we decide to trust in His Word—because it carries His authority.

Hebrews 11:1 gives us this revelation about hope: *"Faith is the assurance of things you have hoped for, the absolute conviction that there are realities you've never seen"* (VOICE version).

Hope strengthens our faith. Hope holds us steady while we live between the now and the future, between the natural and the eternal. God has placed a sense of eternity in our hearts. This gift creates a tension between the now and the what's to come. Our hope is the Lord, who is sovereign over the here and now, and He is the LORD over eternity.

Did you catch that? *"...Hope **IS** the Lord."* So, once again, it is not anything we do to earn anything from Him. It's Him. It's all about Him, all He has done and all He is going to do. Our hope is in Him; He *is* our hope.

"For he shall be like a tree planted by the waters..."

Have you ever seen a tree planted by a stream that never dries up? They are exquisite. They receive all the nutrients they need on a continual basis. They lack for no good thing. Their trunks grow strong and stable. The branches spread out beyond comprehension. The colors they portray are rich and vibrant.

Life-giving waters continually flow, bringing it everything it needs to reach its **full** potential and purpose.

"Which spreads out its roots by the river..."

This is such a beautiful analogy to the importance of having roots in our lives. Too often, we uproot our lives for all the wrong reasons, and we attempt to reestablish ourselves in a new environment. When you uproot a plant incorrectly, it can go into shock; its growth is stunted; it can even reject its new environment.

When we uproot ourselves from relationships, locations and even our church home when it's not what God has asked us to do, the same thing can happen to us. If you left based on unscriptural reasons— running away from something—or you got offended and didn't deal with it scripturally, it follows you. You will still have to deal with anything that doesn't align with the Word of God, or you will repeat the same old cycle.

That, my friend, is not a threat or harsh; it is truth. God wants to transform how you think, speak, and respond to every circumstance in your life. He will keep allowing you to go through life experiences to learn the lesson. We, as Christians, should never leave a relationship, the church God planted us in, or our relationship with Christ, because of offense. We should not be that insecure in who our God is and who we are in Christ.

Roots are interesting things, and different parts of the root have different functions. The main function of roots is to absorb water and minerals to benefit the plant. For you to be healthy, your roots must be absorbing the right nutrients: corporate and private worship; corporate and private prayer; solid Biblical teaching; accountability; fellowship— the Bible is full of what we should be nurturing ourselves with.

Many trees have what is called a taproot. It's a central root that goes deep into the ground, searching for water. They can store food reserves, making them quite resilient to any seasonal changes. For us, in allowing a strong root to be established—a healthy relationship with God and with people—when seasons change in our lives, we have a 'reserve' to help us get through the challenges of those seasons.

Roots will grow in all directions, seeking nutrients and creating a stable anchor for the tree. When the winds come, the tree is anchored. Even when branches break off, the tree can recover. Roots that support and anchor us should not be one-dimensional. Being one-dimensional creates an imbalance in our lives. You can't just have a private prayer life; you need to pray for and with others too. You can't just read the Word; you need to enact the Word as well. You can't just sit on a chair on Sundays; you need to figure out where God wants you to serve. Start somewhere if you have no idea at first; God will direct your steps.

These actions, and so many more, create a root system in our lives that keeps us anchored, feeds us and helps feed (encourage/equip) others.

"And will not fear when heat comes..."

Fear should not be our dominant emotional response to a change in our life circumstance. Fear does have a place as an alarm when danger is approaching. It's like an early warning system. Other kinds of fear do not have a place in a follower of Christ: fear of failure, fear of people, fear of lack, or fear of the outcome of a situation.

"When heat comes" refers to those challenging seasons that come into all our lives. The loss of a job, loss of a loved one, especially an unexpected loss, health issues, divorce, false accusation, or betrayal are all types of *"heat"* we experience in life. But when we are rooted and grounded in the Lord, we have no reason to fear, for we have made the Lord our God our hope and our confidence to strengthen us through the "heat" of life.

"But its leaf will be green..."

God works all things together for good to those who love Him, especially through the challenging and difficult seasons in our lives. If we let Him, and if we remain faithful to Him, He, in His goodness, goes beyond this promise. We, through being planted well, do not have to become weary, exhausted, angry, frustrated, disappointed, or bitter during any season of life.

There are three primary colors—red, yellow and blue—in nature. They cannot be formed through the mixing of other colors. Red is associated with flesh (mankind) and the love of God. Yellow, in the Bible. is associated with fire. Have you heard the expression "trial by fire"? Blue spiritually represents the healing power of God—His Word.

Green is formed by mixing yellow, the trials of life (fire), with blue, healing. God brings healing through every trial of life. The Biblical representation of green is immortality and symbolizes resurrection. Every word in the Word is important, and brings such an explosion of exquisite promises!

Being planted by the streams of living water empowers you to be perpetually brought back to life through the trials of life. Through every trial, bring in the Word of God and you will come out stronger, bolder, with more peace, confidence and joy than you ever believed possible. You will experience growth during every season, and you will enter a new season with an even deeper trust in the faithfulness of the Lord.

"And will not be anxious in the year of drought..."

Like fear, anxiousness should not have a place in our responses towards the seasons in our lives, nor in our state of living. We do not operate from a place of anxiety. When we are planted in the living waters of the Lord, His presence and His Word, we address any circumstance from the promises of God. We operate our lives from a place of trust and peace, not anxiousness, worry or chaos.

So, when the dry seasons come, we are nurtured and refreshed by the presence and Word of God.

"Nor will cease from yielding fruit."

Productivity regardless of the circumstances in your life is possible for the one who is planted in the Truth of God and whose roots are drawing from His promises. Just imagine this!

You've been betrayed by a person you trusted. Your heart is hurt, and your mind is struggling to make sense of it. Fear doesn't enter, because you know fear is not of the Lord. You bring the Word of God into your betrayal, your trial. The Holy Spirit reminds you of how to respond amid a trial, and guides you to the promises of God. In time, the sting of betrayal fades, and restoration flourishes. You produce the fruit of the Spirit in your life: better self-control, greater joy, more peace.

Bitterness, frustration and anger cannot take root and bring destruction because you are planted in deep waters, bringing forth life.

Businesses can weather the trials of worldly recession when they are operating in the promises of God. I also believe that businesses trusting in the Lord God can yield profits in the midst of a recession. God prospers the work of His people, those who are planted in Him. God wants us to bear fruit! He wants us to be productive people, regardless of the season.

Jesus teaches us in John 15 that we are a branch in Him. Jesus is the vine; God is the vinedresser. Every one of us are to bear fruit, or God will remove us. When we do bear fruit, God will prune us to bear even more fruit. We must abide, be planted, in Christ to bear good fruit regardless of the circumstances of our lives or the season we are in (young, middle-aged, older).

We are to produce the good fruit of the Kingdom of God as a testimony of the faithfulness and goodness of the Lord we serve. Good fruit, not bad fruit. We will produce either good or bad fruit, and since God looks at the heart, bad fruit is produced through impure, or self-promoting, self-centered motives.

Producing requires work. Here are some promises pertaining to never ceasing to yield the good fruit of the Lord.

> *"Do you see a man who excels in his work? He will stand before kings; he will not stand before unknown men."* (Proverbs 22:29)

> *"This is a faithful saying, and these things I want you to affirm constantly, that those who have believed in God should be careful to maintain good works. These things are good and profitable to men."* (Titus 3:8)

> *"...And each one will receive His own reward according to his own labor."* (1 Corinthians 3:8)

You need to plant yourself in the things of God that nourish and sustain you, so that your work produces good fruit in all seasons, and proves the good, acceptable and perfect Will of God. Every follower of Christ who wants to live in the abundant life Christ died to give us must plant themselves in principles of God. Then we need to plant ourselves in godly, but specific areas that mature the personal gifts and calling of God upon our lives.

Planting yourself in the ways of God means you can't plant yourself in things contrary to His commands. Scripture is very clear about the consequences one endures and the state one is in when one has one foot in the Kingdom and the other in the world.

> *"For if, after they have escaped the pollutions of the world through the knowledge of the Lord and Savior Jesus Christ, they are again entangled in them and overcome, the latter is worse for them than the beginning. For it would have been better for them not to have known the way of righteousness, than having known it, to turn from the holy commandment delivered to them."* (2 Peter 2:20-21)

Simply put, this verse is saying that once your heart, mind and spirit have experienced the goodness and mercy of God, if you don't keep pursuing Him, you will experience loneliness, confusion, discontentment, frustration, and whatever pain you felt before at a greater intensity than you have ever experienced.

This is because you will be in a constant state of internal conflict. Truth does not coexist with lies. Light does not coexist with darkness. Love does not coexist with hate. Peace does not coexist with chaos. A person in a continual state of internal warring is a person who will be unable to enter into the joy of the Lord.

There are some non-negotiable practices all followers of Christ should be planted in if they want to live out the Kingdom of God here on earth.

Practice the presence of God in every area of your life. God doesn't want just a Sunday relationship. Nor does He want a crisis-only relationship. He desires constant communion with each of us. Genesis 3:8 says, *"And they heard the sound of the LORD God walking in the garden in the cool of the day..."* God was seeking out Adam and Eve to talk with them. It was a common practice, because they recognized His sound. God seeks us out too. But it can't just be a one-way relationship; we must seek Him out. Spend time with Him. Get to know His voice. Experience the overwhelming goodness of His presence.

Learn to live as Jesus lived. Jesus is our aspiration and our example. Every excuse we can come up with to justify not living this life here on earth as Jesus did when He walked this earth can be overruled by the Word of God. We can become overwhelmed by this prospect of having to become like Jesus—primarily, because we take it out of context or put unrealistic expectations on what it means.

We are to cultivate our relationship with Father God above all else. He comes first in our lives. Jesus, even though He is the Son of God, still spent quiet time with the Father.

We are to have the mind of Christ. This is accomplished through the refusal of conforming to the world structure, but being transformed by the renewing of our minds through experiencing God's presence, abiding in Christ, and living out the commands in the Word of God.

We are to be about our Father's business. This may look a little different for each of us as we pursue our individual calling of God and operate in the position and gifts He gives us. But the result is the same: to achieve the great commission Jesus commanded all of us to fulfill in Matthew 28:8-20.

Be Spirit-led. God gave us the Holy Spirit to be our Helper. For various reasons, the Body of Christ does not pursue a relationship with the Person of the Holy Spirit. This, in my opinion, creates a disadvantage in living as Christ calls us to live. Receive the gift of the Holy Spirit. He is not weird; people make Him weird by operating in ignorance or personal agendas. People have also justified disobedience and manipulation of others by the Holy Spirit.

The Holy Spirit will never, ever contradict the Word of God nor the Father's heart. He will also never violate the commands of God, which Jesus summed up by these two commandments: love God and love people.

Be hearers and doers of the Word of God. We are to study and meditate on the Word of God so that His Word does not depart from us and we can live it out. When we do, our ways are made prosperous and we will have good success in our lives.

Cultivate the power of prayer. Jesus prayed; how much more should we? Prayer can be as simple as saying *"Good morning, Lord"* to pulling down strongholds of the enemy. Prayer is one of our greatest gifts and most powerful weapons. Our prayer lives should be rich, joyous and effective.

Fellowship with the brethren (brothers and sisters in Christ). We are to build strong, healthy, fulfilling relationships with other believers. This can be hard in larger churches, but there are ways available to do so. We were meant to live life with others. God is all about relationship. He is all about family. Fellowship with the brethren is meant to bring equipping, encouragement, and accountability to each other.

There are also very few things more glorious to experience than the family of God worshiping and praying together.

It will be impossible to experience the promises found in Jeremiah 17:7-8 without planting yourself in these practices. These lifestyle changes are necessary for you to grow roots, be firmly established, and live a productive and fulfilling life. They are fundamental requirements, not suggestions.

There are other practices each of us need to be planted in, so we are equipped to fulfill our unique calling and utilize the personal gifts God has given us. We will cover this in more detail in the next chapter.

Love God. Love people.

People whose trust is in the Lord and whose hope is the Lord find it easy to love God and to love people. Their identities and validation are not found in the shifting sands of man's opinion. They are constantly validated on who they are based on the firm foundation of the promises of God.

They have firmly planted themselves in the Father's love, the forgiveness and grace of Jesus Christ and the power of the Holy Spirit. They allow themselves to grow to maturity in the principles of God by refusing to tear up and stunt their roots through offense, strife or division. They live a blessed life.

CHAPTER 9

Gifted and Positioned by God

"Now concerning Spiritual Gifts, brethren, I do not want you to be ignorant..." (1 Corinthians 1:1)

God knows you better than anyone else in this world. He formed you with passions, personality traits, intellect, and the ability to reason. He, like any good father, designed you with a beautiful hope and future in mind. He has deposited gifts with you to perfectly equip you for the position(s) He places you in. Not stopping there, He has made available to you the option to earnestly desire, and obtain, the best of His gifts.

As previously discussed, our environments, life choices and experiences can hinder, alter, distort and even destroy the purity of God's desire and purpose for you. But God is relentless in giving you opportunities for complete healing and restoration. The childhood dream may have to be replaced with a different one, but the end result is the same: purpose, fulfilment, peace and joy. All things are possible with God.

I mentioned that my childhood dream was to become a large animal veterinarian, live in the country and raise a very large family. It is highly unlikely that will happen. It's not impossible, though. I could always go back to school, sell our current home, buy land in the country and adopt children. At this stage in my life, however, I simply choose not to pursue that course of action. I choose to allow other dreams to come to life, and I absolutely refuse to live in the past. I personally think it is heartbreaking when I hear people talk about days long past as the best years of their lives.

With God, the best days are available right now, in the present. And with eyes on Jesus, better days are always ahead—not trouble- and trial-free, but abounding in the promises of God. So, I embrace the reality of change and I pursue the utilization of my gifts and positions to fulfill the passions and dreams that the Holy Spirit brings to my heart and mind.

The gifts of God are given to us to glorify God, advance His Kingdom, and to equip us to fulfill His commission through our individual calling… and to bring us great belonging, purpose and fulfillment. When the gifts are not used for their God-given purpose, they can also be a source of discontentment and even our demise.

The same can be said of the positions we fill. The verses we will highlight reference the positions in the Body of Christ. I personally believe that these verses have been used to separate positions in the church from positions outside the church walls. If you are a follower of Christ, then you are a part of the Body of Christ.

Therefore, your gifts and positions are used to fulfill the work of the Kingdom, inside and outside the walls of a church building. You carry the Kingdom of God with you.

There is the five-fold ministry mentioned in Ephesians 4:11:

> *"And He Himself gave some to be apostles, some prophets, some evangelists, and some pastors and teachers…"*

These "offices" are to bring structure and balance to the church. They are appointed by God for the equipping of the saints to edify the Body of Christ. I submit that these positions are just as vital as they have ever been, because if you keep reading, verse 13 says:

> *"…Till we all come to the unity of the faith and of the knowledge of the Son of God, to a perfect man, to the measure of the stature of the fullness of Christ…"*

I will leave it to you and the Holy Spirit to determine your own belief on the five-fold ministry and its relevance today.

I cannot overemphasize the importance of being planted in a church, not just an attender. Followers of Christ should be a faithful and active member of a church body. There is nothing in Scripture that justifies not actively engaging in the vision, equipping, and support of the local church God calls you to and plants you in.

I also believe that God, and the work He calls us to, is not confined to the church walls. As part of the Body of Christ, we carry His Kingdom with us everywhere we go.

A Deeper Look at Giftings

Let's take the traits of apostles, or an apostolic gifting. They are visionary. They take ownership of the vision they have been given. They build relationships with all kinds of people. They have unique insight into the abilities and giftings of others. They have little fear of starting things from scratch and the challenges that may bring. They want to grow things and be successful. They require little external motivation, and they have an above-normal 'bounce-back ability'. Failure is not a deterrent; in fact, it's often a motivator.

Do you know who else these traits remind me of? Entrepreneurs.

Webster's dictionary defines an entrepreneur as *"a person who organizes and operates a business or businesses, taking on greater than normal financial risks in order to do so."* I submit that they take on more risk period, not just financial. They are gifted and called to create something from nothing. These incredible men and women have an innate desire to bring forth and establish. Their passion tends to fade once a business is operating well; they begin to pursue a new vision.

The good news is that there are people who are gifted and called to operations, listed Spiritually as administration. When apostolic and administration-gifted people have embraced their gifts and position, nothing is held back. However, when fear, insecurity, covetousness has a place in either position, it brings strife, division and, if not corrected, the painful and harmful kind of failure.

Let's look at the gifting and positions of craftsman and artisans. The world, unfortunately including some who profess Christ as Savior, demeans the exquisite gifts and positions of crafts. The ability to carry crafts and technical skills is a gift of God.

> *"Then the LORD spoke to Moses, saying: 'See, I have called by name Bezalel the son of Uri, the son of Hur, of the tribe of Judah. And **I have filled him with the Spirit of God, in wisdom, in understanding, in knowledge, and in all manner of workmanship, to design artistic works, to work in gold, in silver, in bronze, in cutting jewels for setting, in carving wood, and to work in all manner of workmanship.** And I, indeed I, have appointed with him Aholiab the son of Ahisamach,*

*of the tribe of Dan; and **I have put wisdom in the hearts of all the gifted artisans, that they may make all that I have commanded you...**"* (Exodus 31:1-6, emphasis added)

Isn't that extraordinary!? God filled these men with His Spirit and the gifts needed to complete all He had commanded Moses to accomplish. He gifted and positioned Moses one way. He also gifted and positioned others in other ways to accomplish God's plan. Every person had a role to fulfill, a work to be done. Every person was just as important as the other. For without them working together, I think Moses would have not been able to fulfill God's command. The beauty is that, when the work was done, EVERYONE BENEFITED, because the glory of God filled the tent.

We waste so much time and effort wishing we had other gifts or another position than the one we are in. If we allow the healing needed to take place, embrace the gifts we have, and be content with the position we are currently in, there is no limit to what God could accomplish in and through us.

Have you heard the expression "They have the gift of gab?" Do you know someone who has never met a stranger? Or has a way with numbers that makes your head spin? Or those who have a way with words? Create a beautiful work of art from clay? Play music with minimal lessons? Love to connect people?

All these and so much more speak to the gifts and positions of God. And they are intended to work together, not against each other or in competition.

The Holy Spirit is our Teacher to help us embrace, develop and operate in the gifts and position(s) God has called us to. We need Him to operate as our Helper and Teacher in these matters, or the likelihood of disappointment, frustration and the abuse of the gifts highly increases.

Begin to Fully Embrace and Operate in Your Gifts

Pursue the gift-Giver and His Kingdom above pursuing the gifts and position. The greatest commandment tells us to love the Lord our God with all our heart, all our soul, all our strength and all our mind. The gifts and positions of God can become an idol, a source of pride and, even more harmful, your source of validation and self-worth. God is your Source.

You need to continually learn to hide your life in Christ. This means, in a short sentence, you give up your agenda, for His. You give up self-promotion for Christ-exaltation. This doesn't mean being a doormat; it means you recognize that apart from Christ, anything you produce is short-lived and unfruitful. Our lives are hidden with Christ in God (Colossians 3:3).

You must be Spirit-led. The Holy Spirit searches the deep things of God and reveals them to us. It is His responsibility to bring revelation and understanding to who we are, our gifts, and what God is preparing for us. He is our conviction when our heart is not right. He brings correction when we step out of bounds. Correctly operating in the gifts of God requires the Holy Spirit.

Put on the armor of God. We must always remember we have a real enemy—satan. The armor of God protects us and allows us to do battle WITH the Lord against the real enemy. We will discuss the armor of God in more detail in an upcoming chapter.

Do not neglect the gift that is in you. Neglecting the gifts within you, and those God has for you, will leave you with emptiness and unfulfillment. You were meant to operate in the gifts of God!

Never forget the purpose of Spiritual Gifts. They are for:

- **The profit of all** (1 Corinthians 12:7).

- **The health and growth of the Body of Christ** *(in and out of the church walls)* (Ephesians 4:16).

- **The Edification of the Church** (1 Corinthians 14:12).

- **Each of us to fit rightly and fulfill our positions, roles, in the Body of Christ** (1 Corinthians 12:20-26).

- **Above all, to serve God** (Romans 12:1-3).

If they are being used for other or self-serving motives, they will not bear the satisfaction and fulfilment they are intended for. If you constantly pursue positions God doesn't desire for you, you will feel frustrated and dissatisfied.

I know this from personal experience. I begged God to allow me to be put in a certain position. The Holy Spirit kept telling me I really didn't want it. But I kept asking. Finally, God allowed it to happen. And... I... was... MISERABLE! It took a while to get out of that one. Before He allowed me out, I had to acknowledge and repent of what

I had done—and embrace the reality that *I* had chosen it, and I had kept bombarding God with what I wanted. God didn't want it for me, because He knew what it would do to me. I learned a very valuable lesson; God knows best for me. He truly is my Abba Father.

Scripture, as always, instructs us on how we are supposed to operate in the gifts and positions of God. The Holy Spirit gives us the revelation and teaches us how to accomplish it. 1 Corinthians 12 provides this instruction:

> *"There are diversity of gifts, but the same Spirit. There are difference of ministries, but the same Lord. And there are diversity of activities, but it is the same God who works all in all."* (Verses 4-6)

The diversity of the gifts, difference of ministries and diversity of activities SHOULD be directed by the same Spirit, Lord and God. However, what do we often find? A lack of discipleship in understanding the gifts. A lack of maturity in comprehending that there are more things at work than your personal passion (gift, ministry, or activity).

A person who has not been healed of past hurts tries to find their worth and validation by their gift or through their position.

These, and other self-driven motives, bring division, strife, offense, anger, and bitterness into the work of the Kingdom and hinder the productivity a Spirit-, Lord-, God-led people can yield.

> *"But one and the same Spirit works all these things, distributing to each one individually as He Wills."* (Verse 11)

The Spirit is constantly working towards unity in the Body for the glory of God. It is He who distributes the gifts according to GOD'S WILL. This means it is not your Lead Pastor who gifts you. It also isn't you who gifts and positions you. It is God, and only God, who gets the credit. So, if you're envious of another person's gift or position, you may want to do a heart check. You may be the one holding yourself back from experiencing the joy of working together as a Body.

> *"For in fact the body is not one member but many. If the foot should say, "Because I am not a hand, I am not of the body," is it therefore not of the body? And if the ear should say, "Because I am not an eye, I am not of the body," is it therefore not of the body? If the whole body were an eye, where would be the hearing? If the whole were hearing, where would be the smelling? But now God has set the members, each one of*

them, in the body just as He pleased. And if they were all one member, where would the body be?" (Verses 14-19)

Isn't God brilliant? He has designed the Body of Christ to need, dare I say, to be dependent upon each other (in a healthy way). And He diversified the 'parts' so that, to be at our best, we MUST learn to work together.

We miss the glory of the Body because we are too absorbed in our individual part and what our part does for us, rather than "How do I mature in my part so the whole Body benefits?" Our perspective needs to change and find validation and joy in the truth that our part helps complete the Body and without us, the Body doesn't function as it's designed by God to. Our part matters!

We are overcomers in Christ. There isn't any life too broken that God can't restore. Unfortunately, we allow God to heal our pain, but we resist allowing Him to mature us to operate in His gifts and steward the position He desires for us well. This leaves a gap that others often have to fill that they are not called to. Because they love the Lord, when they see a need, they fill it—but if they are in there too long, weariness and unfulfillment is not far behind.

The gifts are meant to be used in conjunction with others' gifts, so the greater goal is accomplished: Christ is exalted, and people are set free. Each position is meant to complement the other, so the work is spread out, we don't grow weary, and there isn't division in the Body of Christ. It brings UNITY! And it reduces the likelihood of pride and selfishness taking root.

God just outdoes His genius on this next Truth.

> *"But now indeed there are many members, yet one body. And the eye cannot say to the hand, "I have no need of you"; nor again the head to the feet, "I have no need of you." No, much rather, those members of the body which seem to be weaker are necessary. And those members of the body which we think to be less honorable, on these we bestow greater honor; and our unpresentable parts have greater modesty, but our presentable parts have no need. But God composed the body, having given greater honor to that part which lacks it."* (Verses 20-24)

Read and meditate on His genius again.

The eye, hand and head are very visible parts of the Body. They get noticed and praised. People compliment them, bring them gift cards, and send them thank-you notes. But those poor feet, knees, elbows and hips don't get too much attention… *until something goes wrong.* You will quickly learn how vital those feet, knees, elbows and hips are. It's like when your pinky finger gets smashed—you soon learn how much that little fellow is used and needed.

Those of us who are blessed with "behind the scenes" gifts and positions may struggle with a lack of being appreciated. We see the visible parts being encouraged and spoken life into, and our flesh and/or the enemy can twist that moment to: "Well, what about me?"; "No one around here appreciates what I do". If those thoughts are not taken captive and replaced with the truth that God has bestowed greater honor on those "parts that lack it", then you've just allowed your joy to be stolen.

Each of us has individual responsibility to make sure we are not seeking validation and deriving our self-worth from man. We also have a responsibility to make sure we are encouraging and honoring every gift and every part of the Body.

> *"But God composed the body, having given greater honor to that part which lacks it, that there should be no schism in the body, but that the members should have the same care for one another. And if one member suffers, all the members suffer with it; or if one member is honored, all the members rejoice with it."* (Verses 24b-26)

Simply GENIUS! Now, if only we, God's people, can allow His brilliance to be actively working in our lives. Can you imagine the results? Oh, how glorious it would be!

Be on guard against legalism with the gifts and positions of God. God is more than capable of allowing you to operate in any gift in any position He needs you to in order to accomplish what HE desires to be accomplished.

My natural inclination is more introvert than extrovert. Me, myself, I and Jesus are perfectly content all by ourselves. I can go for days without interacting with people and be at perfect peace. Yes, I do love people and I enjoy bringing people together. In my dream world, though, I'd bring people together, make sure everyone was okay, then slip out the back door to return for clean-up. I can become drained by large groups of people. Knowing this about myself, and taught by the Holy Spirit, I can still operate in the gift of hospitality. But wisdom and self-care dictates that I have to refill. Quietness fills me up. I can't operate in hospitality all the time because I need to operate in the dominant

118

gifts and positions God has called me to. I'm more effective in those areas because I'm where God positioned me.

I share this because sometimes we can get very rigid with the gifts of God. We use them as an excuse not to be a blessing or meet an immediate need. "I can't do that because it's not my gifting!" Paul tells us:

> *"I can do all things through Christ who strengthens me."* (Philippians 4:13)

Paul learned how to be content in any situation/position he was in because he knew God was ordering his steps. Paul also operated in what he needed to in order to accomplish the greater goal of the Good News of Jesus Christ. This didn't make him a hypocrite, because his motivation was love. He knew that for him to be able to reach a person/people, he had to first interact with them at a level they could relate to. No, this doesn't mean you have to get drunk to relate to a person who battles with alcohol: it means don't box God in.

He is just as relentless to restore others as He was to restore you. The difference is, you get to be a part of His work. So, again, don't box God's gifts and positions in. He often likes to color outside the lines. Since He is God, He can. Your guidelines/boundaries in meeting people where they are at, or operating in God's gifts: if they violate Scripture, stop coloring.

The gifts of God are exquisite. They are powerful. They change lives. They move mountains. We are encouraged to *"earnestly desire"* the best gifts. So, go for it—earnestly desire the gifts of God.

But if you want excellence, and to live a brilliant life, the greatest gift you can earnestly desire is love. Desire to love and be loved by God so you can love yourself and love others... and be loved by them. It is difficult to receive love when wounds still guard our hearts.

The operation of any gift, if not motivated by and done in love, amounts to nothing.

Paul says it best in 1 Corinthians 13:1-3:

> *"Though I speak with the tongues of men and of angels, but have not love, I have become sounding brass or a clanging cymbal. And though I have the gift of prophecy, and understand all mysteries and all knowledge, and though I have all faith, so that I could remove mountains, but have not love, I am nothing.*

And though I bestow all my goods to feed the poor, and though I give my body to be burned, but have not love, it profits me nothing."

Everything, once again, boils down to love. Love God and receive His love. Receive His love and you can love people. His love will transform your heart, and love will be your motivation to accomplish more than you can ever think or imagine. Love conquers. Love overcomes.

The primary Spiritual Gifts references are found in Romans 12:3-9, 1 Corinthians 12, 1 Peter 4:10-11. But don't limit yourself to this list; other gifts of God are listed throughout His Word. There are excellent books that you can do an in-depth study of the Gifts on. I encourage you to start with the Holy Bible, with your teacher the Holy Spirit. I've listed several gifts here with their corresponding Scripture reference. They are not listed in order of importance.

Word of wisdom (1 Corinthians 12:8; Luke 6:9).

Word of knowledge (1 Corinthians 12:8; Luke 18:22).

Faith (1 Corinthians 12:9; Acts 3:6).

Gifts of healing (1 Corinthians 12:9, 28; Acts 28:1-10).

Working of miracles (1 Corinthians 12:10; Acts 6:8).

Prophecy (1 Corinthians 12:10; 1 Thessalonians 5:20-21; Ephesians 4:11).

Discerning of spirits (1 Corinthians 12:10; Luke 8:29).

Tongues (1 Corinthians 12:10, 28; Acts 19:6).

Interpretation of tongues (1 Corinthians 12:10; 14:13-33).

Helping (1 Corinthians 12:28).

Administration (1 Corinthians 12:28; Acts 6:2-3).

Ministry/service (Romans 12:7; 2 Timothy 1:16-18).

Teaching (Romans 12:7; Ephesians 4:11-14).

Encouragement (Rom. 12:8; Hebrews 10:24-25).

Giving (Romans 12:8; 1 Corinthians 13:3; Acts 4:32-35).

Leadership (Romans 12:8; Acts 13:12).

Mercy (Romans 12:8; Luke 5:12-13).

Apostleship (Ephesians 4:11).

Evangelism (Ephesians 4:11; 2 Tim. 4:5).

Pastoral guidance/shepherding (Ephesians 4:11).

Grace (Romans 12:6; Ephesians 3:7; 4:7; 1 Peter 4:10-11).

Willingness to face martyrdom (1 Corinthians 13:3).

Intercession (Romans 8:26-27).

Hospitality (1 Peter 4:9).

Celibacy (1 Corinthians 7:8).

It is important to consistently do heart checks regarding the gifts and the positions God gives us. What God means for good can be turned into a tool for the enemy to bring about our downfall. All you do should be motivated by your love for God and by your love for others… and don't forget to take care of yourself. It's not selfish; it's wise and Scriptural.

Remember also that what the enemy means for evil, God is more than able to turn to good. So do not be fearful of making mistakes, getting it wrong, experiencing whatever stumble may happen as you practice operating in the gifts of God. God's grace covers 'oops' moments when they were committed with hearts motived by love. God's grace does not cover continual rebellion, disorderly conduct, or selfish motives. Please don't think you can fool God. He knows your heart.

Spiritual Gifts produce Spiritual Fruit, and Spiritual Fruit enlarges Spiritual Gifts. A powerful indicator that you are operating as God desires you to in His Spiritual Gifts is that the Fruit of the Spirit is being produced in and by your life.

"But the fruit of the Spirit is love, joy, peace, longsuffering, kindness, goodness, faithfulness, gentleness, self-control. Against such there is no law." (Galatians 5:22)

As this 'fruit' become more obvious in your life, the effectiveness (power, authority) of the gifts are also increased. The reason is, you are allowing your heart and mind to be transformed into the heart and mind of Christ. Therefore, God can trust you to a greater level to steward His gifts well.

Additionally, as you mature, He knows the gifts won't become a stumbling block in your life. He knows you are zealous for spiritual gifts for the elevation of the church, and not for selfish gain.

I encourage you to study Scripture on how the gifts are to be used on an individual and in a corporate environment—particularly the gifts of tongues and prophecy. Of all the gifts, these two have been misused, abused and used to manipulate and control others the most. They are also the dominant ones used to promote and glorify the person using the gifts. You are not the Holy Spirit police, nor God's watchdog. But you are called to "know people by their fruit," and all followers of Christ can operate in discernment.

Too many followers of Christ chase after the gifts, or those operating in the gifts, rather than chasing after God, the One who gives the gift.

Equip yourself through your own study of Scripture first, then continue to equip yourself through Bible Studies about Spiritual Gifts. Scripture is very clear on the purpose and operation of these powerful gifts. Don't be drawn into silly debates or allow yourself to be a source of strife and division. The Holy Spirit will tell you what to do and say. He usually tells me to quote Scripture and then let Him work it out with others. Be a peacemaker.

God has gifted you! So pursue those gifts, mature in them, and use them for your and others' good. Operate in them for His glory. God has positioned you, so embrace the position He has you in. It may or may not be your destination, but one thing I know—if you do not learn what He needs you to learn, you're not going anywhere. You may quit, but you'll never advance internally or externally. You'll spend your life in a stalemate. That's not what God desires for you. He wants you ever growing in your favor with Him and man.

Remember, the gifts and positions of God are wonderful. But abiding in faith, hope and love are beyond measure. And the greatest of these is love. Serve well, but love better!

CHAPTER 10

Weapons of Our Warfare

"For though we walk in the flesh, we do not war according to the flesh." (2 Corinthians 10:3)

We have a real enemy, and his sole purpose is to steal, kill and destroy lives. He thought higher of higher than he ought, rebelled against God, and does everything he can to corrupt and destroy God's creation, including us. God has made His truth known and through Jesus Christ, He has made us free. We have access to life, and life more abundantly.

But make no mistake, we are still in a battle. The good news is, God has given us the weapons we need to do battle and come out victorious — we fight with the confidence that the final battle has already been won through Christ, and we are on the winning side.

Our greatest weapon in this war is our relationship with the Father, Son and Holy Spirit. Jesus Christ, who is the way, the truth and the life, has won the battle of reconciliation to our Creator and over death. Through Him, we are made right before God. Therefore, when we are facing a battle, we are to fight in it by God's terms and using His weapons.

The primary battlegrounds for us are in the mind and in the heart. The entry points for having to do battle on those grounds are the eyes and the ears. These entry points are a gateway for the flesh to be tempted and rise up. Temptation does not come from God; it comes from our own selfish desires and wants, not needs. If not dealt with at the onslaught, desire gives birth to sin, and when sin is allowed to grow, it will bring forth death.

The quickest way to win a battle is to end it before it begins.

The most powerful weapon we have is Truth. God's Truth will prevail. Always. God's Word is the weapon that reveals the foolishness of philosophies and tears down arguments trying to disprove His Truth.

> *"For though we walk in the flesh, we do not war according to the flesh. For the weapons of our warfare are not carnal but mighty in God for pulling down strongholds, casting down arguments and every high thing that exalts itself against the knowledge of God, bringing every thought into captivity to the obedience of Christ, and being ready to punish all disobedience when your obedience is fulfilled."* (2 Corinthians 10:3-6)

To win the war before the battle begins, you train yourself to take every thought captive and bring it to the obedience of Christ. If you see something that contradicts the Word of God, you avert your eyes before it forms a thought in your mind. If the thought is formed, you take the thought captive, repent, ask for forgiveness and replace it with a Truth from God's Word. Then, you MOVE FORWARD.

Yes, it is that simple.

It is the same with what you hear. If what you are listening to distorts or contradicts the Word of God, you reject it by confronting it with God's Truth. There is no need for debate or proving through arguments the validity of God's Word. You simply need to stand on it and live it out. That will be testimony enough to others of its soundness.

The enemy has been watching and influencing man for a very long time. I do not believe he can read minds, but I do believe he knows man, and he and his minions watch our behavior. They seize opportunities, prey on our weaknesses and use every means possible to entice us away from Truth. One of the enemy's tactics is to twist, even if it's to the tiniest of degrees, the Word of God. The enemy did it with Adam and Eve; he even tried it with Jesus Christ in the wilderness. So, then, wisdom would dictate that he will use the same tactic with you.

You must know the Word of God. Otherwise, you are easily led astray and deceived. I do not have the entire Word of God memorized, but I know enough of the Word and Heart of God to know when something is not of God. We also have the Holy Spirit to let us know. The Holy Spirit will alert us to when something isn't in alignment with God. But to be sensitive to His prompting, you must be familiar to His voice.

The enemy cannot make you do anything. The excuse of "the devil made me do it," will not stand, nor will "I just couldn't help myself." God has provided you weapons to guard yourself and remove yourself from moving into sin.

The most powerful weapon you have is living your life according to the commands of God. When you pursue a life in Christ, the promises of God are activated in your life. Therefore, He fights for you. When you live your life in the flesh, according to your desires, you fight battles on your own strength... which is ineffective and exhausting.

Romans 12:19 instructs us to not avenge ourselves, but to allow latitude for the Lord's wrath. If we take matters into our own hands to right a wrong committed against us, then we have forfeited room for God to interject Himself into the process. We have brought justice at a human level instead of trusting God to bring His justice to both parties involved.

Luke 6:28 encourages us to bless those who curse us and pray for those who spitefully use us.

Romans 12:21 teaches us to not be overcome by evil, but we are to overcome evil with good... again, not our definition of good, but God's.

These, and other truths, are the weapons God has given us to be made free.

The first nine verses of Ephesians 6 are the weapons of our warfare. Children are to obey their parents. Parents are not to provoke their children to wrath. Bondservants, which, I propose, could be applied to employees in today's time, are to be good employees, not as men-pleasers, but as Christ-followers. Everything followers of Christ do is unto the Lord, to please Him and bring glory to His name. Masters, employers, are to treat their employees well, knowing there is no partiality with God.

Then we get into the armor of God we are to wear every day. Our armor should become part of who we are.

"Finally, my brethren, be strong in the Lord and in the power of His might." There is no being stronger than the Lord. There is no authority higher than His. And there is no one mightier. You need to build yourself up in Him. Strengthen yourself in His presence and in His Word. You must continually follow His commands and live out His promises.

> *"Put on the whole armor of God, that you may be able to stand against the wiles of the devil. For we do not wrestle against flesh*

and blood, but against principalities, against powers, against the rulers of the darkness of this age, against spiritual hosts of wickedness in the heavenly places." (Ephesians 6:10-12)

Put on the **whole armor** of God. You can't just put on a partial armor and expect to be protected. I was playing hide and seek with my five-year-old granddaughter the other day. She sat in the middle of the floor, tucked herself into a ball and pulled an oversized T-shirt over herself. She thought that because she couldn't see me, I couldn't see her. But there she was, in plain sight, fully exposed to a full-on "attack" from her grandma. Now, while I *tickled* my granddaughter, the enemy will use any opening you allow to *destroy* you.

You can't have Jesus in your heart, and then ignore having your mind transformed. Battles are won and lost in the mind. Your mind cannot be left exposed to the trickery and deceit of the enemy. If left unguarded, eventually, your mind will influence your heart and turn you away from Jesus Christ.

The opposite is also true. You can know every Scripture through memorization, but if your heart is not renewed through the Spirit, you just know words. They will not produce the fullness of fruit God has available. Yes, some fruit will be produced, because it's God's Word, and He backs up His Word. But you will not experience the fullness of the promise.

Our battle isn't with other people. Our battle, the war, is against our own flesh, which is fully in our control if we take ownership of it. 1 Corinthians 6:12-20 also gives instruction regarding the flesh. Our choices are our own responsibility to bring our flesh, personal desires, under control. We have been given freedom in Christ, but we shouldn't use that freedom to do whatever we want. Having no self-control puts us in bondage to our whims. Whims are rarely, if ever, profitable.

Our battle is with the enemy, with principalities, powers, rulers of the darkness of the age and against spiritual hosts of wickedness. Only the weapons God has provided us with will give us victory over such foes.

"Therefore take up the whole armor of God, that you may be able to withstand in the evil day, and having done all, to stand." We must take up the whole armor of God in order to be able to withstand evil. Once we do, we are to stand. We are not to stand in our own power and might, but we are to stand, and stand firmly, in God's authority and His power. He is the One standing behind His Word.

We are to stand with our waist girded with God's Truth. The waist is the center of the body, and it provides balance and strength to the rest of the body. When it is off-center, the rest of the body is off-center. God's Truth holds everything together. We must have a sincere trust in the faithfulness of our God. We are to stand in God's Truth, through every circumstance and battle. We stand in God's Truth in order to respond to every situation with grace, goodness, and confidence.

We put on the Breastplate of Righteousness. The righteousness of Christ protects our hearts. Our lives are hidden in Christ. Our sins are forgiven through Him. We have been made right with God because of our belief, our faith, that Jesus Christ is our Lord and Savior. If we doubt this Truth, then our heart is exposed to the darts of the enemy, so we must stand in the righteousness found in Christ Jesus and guard our hearts.

Our feet are shod with the preparation of the Gospel of Peace. We must know the Gospel of Peace in order to live out peace. Peace doesn't mean an absence of trials. Jesus said we will have trials and tribulations; but He also said we can have peace in the midst of every storm. In order to have peace, we must know the Good News of Jesus Christ. Every step we take is meant to bring the Gospel of Jesus Christ into the territory. We are to be able to be sure-footed in the peace of God, regardless of the terrain.

We take up the Shield of Faith in order to quench ALL the fiery darts of the wicked one (satan). "Take up" is an action—therefore it requires an intentional choice. We can't put down and pick up our faith whenever it is needed or convenient. Our faith must be evident every moment of every day. Faith is required to resist temptation. Faith is required to protect oneself and others we care about. Our faith is our shield.

The Helmet of Salvation protects our minds. Salvation keeps our minds pure and sets it on things above, not on things of the earth. We are to use our minds to meditate on things that are true, noble, just, pure, lovely and of good report. Our minds should be focused on virtuous things and things that are praiseworthy. If we focus on such matters, then our minds are too filled to focus on other things. I can promise you this: if you look, you can find God's goodness in every situation. I am not one to stick my head in the sand and ignore the reality of a situation. I'm a firm believer in recognizing things as they are, but calling them to become as they should be, as defined by God's Word.

The Sword of the Spirit, which is the Word of God. The Word of God is a weapon of attack. Every other item listed is defense. A single verse of Scripture, when well understood and rightly applied, disarms every lie, distortion, and desire, and subdues the enemy under the feet of Jesus Christ. 'Well understood' and 'rightly applied' are very important. We can't manipulate Scripture to accomplish our own selfish desires or self-promoting agendas. Our motives must be pure and Kingdom-minded. God is not mocked. He knows our hearts; therefore, He knows our motives.

Then there is prayer. Prayer is both a weapon of attack and a weapon of defense. We must have a healthy and active prayer life. We turn to prayer in times of distress, but most of us fail to maintain an ongoing prayer discipline in our daily lives. If our prayer life is continual, and we are engaged in all types of prayer, then when difficult seasons arise, we are prepared. The entire next chapter is dedicated to the gift and power of prayer. If you want to be made free, then your prayer life must become as important to you as breathing.

1 Peter 5:6-10 and James 4:7-10 both give instruction on submitting to God and resisting the devil, which will cause the enemy to flee. This is another weapon of our warfare. We must humble ourselves and remove pride from our lives. Humbling ourselves does not make us weak. Humbling ourselves actually makes us stronger, because we do not live in our strength, but in God's.

God resists the proud, but He gives grace to the humble. Humbling means we have an understanding that we need God. Humbling means that we understand that regardless of ethnicity, economic status, or even degree of sin evident in our lives, we are no better nor worse than anyone else.

We are to be sober: which means we are to not be mad, insane, wild or heated with passion, but exercise cool, dispassionate reason. We should have a level head about us. We are to be vigilant: to be watchful and attentive, to discover and AVOID danger. Did you catch that? We are more than able to be level-headed and attentive in order to AVOID DANGER. When we are too busy, too distracted and not putting into practice the tools and weapons God has provided to us, we are easy pickings for the enemy.

When we are sober and vigilant, we are on guard to resist the devil, who is walking about like a roaring lion, seeking whom he may devour. Resisting the devil will cause him to flee, but we must resist him in the might and power of the Lord.

Our greatest weapon is found in the sincerity and depths of our relationship with Father God. It is knowing who our Savior is and who we are in Him. It is pursuing and living a Holy Spirit-led life, rooted and grounded in the Word of God.

We cannot be double-minded in our faith. We cannot have one foot in the Kingdom and one foot in the world. It makes us unstable in all of our ways; it makes us easy targets for the enemy to derail and devour us.

Every trial, every temptation, every difficulty is an opportunity to be built up in your faith. Through each of those circumstances, we grow in boldness and confidence in the goodness and faithfulness of our God. Every situation produces patience, and learning how to be patient is a glorious work that makes us perfect and complete.

You are an overcomer. You have been given weapons by God to live free and victorious. If you feel under-equipped in any of these areas, ask God to grow you in these areas. God desires to give His children what they need to live the life He has for them as a joint heir with Christ.

Ask, and believe you have received, and you will come out victorious through every battle. You have everything you need in the arsenal of Almighty God.

CHAPTER 11

Prayer is Not Optional

"For this reason we also, since the day we heard it, do not cease to pray for you, and to ask that you may be filled with the knowledge of His will in all wisdom and spiritual understanding..." (Colossians 1:9)

Prayer at its most intimate is having an open and honest conversation with God. Prayer at its most powerful changes the destinies of people and nations. A healthy, continual, effective prayer life is essential to a follower of Christ. Prayer is not optional.

The importance, power, and effectiveness of prayer is evident throughout Scripture. There is story after story of how people prayed, individually and corporately, and God moved on their behalf in miraculous ways. Scripture records that Jesus Christ Himself would often go off alone to pray. If Jesus, the Son of God, prayed, how much more should we?

Scripture instructs us to have a prayer life that is unceasing (1 Thessalonians 5:17). It also tells us to be anxious for nothing, but in all things through prayer, supplication, with thanksgiving, to make our requests known to God (Philippians 4:6). But, next to tithing, it is probably one of the most difficult disciplines to maintain in our lives. Why? Because if the enemy can keep us from praying, he knows we are not a force to be concerned about.

The two biggest obstacles to cultivating an unceasing prayer life are ourselves and, of course, the enemy. The enemy's tactics include but are not limited to condemnation (in the form of accusation that you're not good enough to pray, not worthy, etc.), distraction, busyness, and lies. Every one of the tactics the enemy uses, we use as well to justify not sustaining a healthy prayer life.

Every one of those lies and excuses can be overcome through making a choice that prayer will be a priority and applying discipline to make it a reality. We need to understand that when we seek the Kingdom of God first and His righteousness, all these things will be added to us (Matthew 6). 'All things' refers to all the things you need, not want, in your life.

I was in a mentoring session with a young lady who was in crisis. She made the comment that she was too embarrassed to pray because she hadn't prayed in such a long time. This is a lie of the enemy, and it's a justification of the flesh. God hears the cries of His people, always. So never let any excuse, nor any state you are in, stop you from crying out to God.

God wants more than just to talk to you in times of crisis, though. He desires to have ongoing communion with you. He also wants to entrust you with His Will being done on earth as it is in heaven. He, through His Spirit, desires to use you to intervene in the lives of the broken-hearted and give them an opportunity to change their destinies for their good and His glory.

The reality is, if we just cultivated a life of prayer, all the provision of heaven would be at our disposal. Provision is not limited to material needs; it includes the spiritual provision we so desperately need and unknowingly hunger for.

Prayer is the conduit that activates the Truth and Will of God in our lives and the world. We have made it so incredibly complicated, and it truly isn't. Prayer is a beautiful, joyous, overwhelming and powerful gift. There are many different types of prayer, and they all begin and end in relationship with the Father.

You nurture a relationship with the Father through prayer, and through prayer, He nurtures you.

Personal Prayer

"But you, when you pray, go into your room, and when you have shut your door, pray to your Father who is in the secret place; and your Father who sees in secret will reward you openly. And

132

when you pray, do not use vain repetitions as the heathens do. For they think that they will be heard for their many words." (Matthew 6:6-7)

We are to have a private, personal, one-on-one prayer life. There are no hard and fast rules to this other than how Jesus instructs us not to use ineffective repetitions. These are protocols, not legalism or a checklist, but an honoring of the Lord in prayer. The Model Prayer in Mathew 6:13 reveals some of these protocols: acknowledging the Lord our God as holy; prayer being about His Will, not ours being done; trusting Him for our provision; forgiveness of our sins as we forgive others; and continual deliverance from temptation. The prayer ends with the declaration that the Kingdom, power and glory belongs to God, and God alone. We are His children, and joint-heirs, co-laborers with Christ.

Prayer is not about jumping in and telling God what you need, what to do and how to do it. It's not all about you. It's honoring Him, spending time with Him and building a relationship. It's about learning about Him, hearing His voice, being forever changed by being in His presence. And that's just the tip of the iceberg.

I am not a morning person. I like moving at my own pace, and I don't like to talk. So I'm not one of those people who wakes up at 3AM and starts praying... unless the Holy Spirit wakes me up.

But before I roll out of bed, I pray. It's not eloquent. It may not feel very powerful or effective. Sometimes it could equate to a page in a book; other times, a paragraph. I've even had it as short as a sentence. I usually pray something like this when I wake up grumpy: "This is the day that the Lord has made, and I will rejoice and be glad." When I have a busy day ahead: "Holy Spirit, let's do this day." Regardless, before my feet hit the ground, I have thanked and asked the Lord to be a part of His day, and I have invited Him to be a part of mine.

Throughout my day, I pray. Let's simplify that. Throughout my day, I talk to the Lord. I include Him in every aspect of my life. When someone enters my office, I quickly ask the Holy Spirit to give me wisdom. If I'm dealing with a work error, I ask Him to reveal where the error is. I ask Him if I need to apologize, confront, deal with something, be quiet... then I say thank you. I make conscious choices to keep Him in the midst of my day.

I spend time with the Lord. Sometimes I just sit in His presence to soak and listen. Other times, I do a lot of talking. My husband and I were clearing some land and I saw an image in my head of Jesus and me sitting on a certain bench, overlooking the pond. So I made a bench, and when we go out to the land, I sit on that bench and imagine that Jesus is sitting next to me. Sometimes we talk; sometimes we just sit together. To some that might sound weird, but for me, it's a physical reminder that the Lord is closer than a brother. He has promised to never leave me nor forsake me.

A personal prayer life secures you in your relationship with the Father, Son, and Holy Spirit. A personal prayer life activates the Holy Spirit to be able to tell you of things to come so you'll be prepared. A personal prayer life allows the Lord to perfect those things that concern you in the privacy of your life. This is much easier than the Lord having to deal with things in your life publicly. God's heart is to deal with things privately, but He will go public if we refuse to address the issue. He is more concerned with your heart than He is with your public reputation.

A personal prayer life builds trust between you and the Lord. He will be able to entrust you with His power and authority at greater levels to move mountains, intercede on others' behalf, and fight battles in the spiritual realm so they do not manifest in the natural. This means the victory is won in the spiritual realm, and those in the natural realm only see the outcome of that battle.

Nurture a personal prayer life. It is the cornerstone of a life in Christ. A personal prayer life unlocks the keys of heaven.

Corporate Prayer

Corporate prayer simply means followers of Christ coming together and praying to the Father. It doesn't matter the number of people. It can be as few as two, or in the tens of thousands. What matters is the sincerity of heart to pursue Jesus Christ and not a personal agenda. Followers of Christ are to gather together in the Lord's name, not in our names.

> "For where two or three are gathered together in My name, I am there in the midst of them." (Mathew 18:20)

This goes for personal prayer too.

> James 5:16: "...the effective, fervent prayers of a righteous man (woman) avails much."

> 1 Peter 3:12: "For the eyes of the Lord are on the righteous, And His ears are open to their prayers..."

Righteous is to be right with God. It means to be holy in heart and observant of the commands of God. Not perfect, but the driving force is to love God and to love others.

There is an order to corporate prayer. It is not chaotic, but it should be orchestrated by the Holy Spirit and have a flow to it. Corporate prayer is not confusing. For new followers of Christ, there may be a lack of understanding of what may be happening, especially if the Gifts of the Spirit are active. But there should never be confusion. God is not the author of confusion, but of peace.

Confusion and chaos can occur when people allow envy to enter and are seeking to be heard or noticed. Scripture says to let all things to be done decently and in order.

Corporate prayer should have a leader. This is not to control, but to facilitate the prayer time. Others should honor the authority of the leader and pray according to instruction. This brings unity. If the Holy Spirit needs to bring something up to be prayed for, then this too can be done in an orderly fashion, and without quenching the Spirit.

Corporate prayer is extraordinary when the people come together in one accord to pray and worship. Prayer and worship often go hand-in-hand. As a follower of Jesus Christ, you need to participate in corporate prayer at your church or other events. Prayer is not a spectator sport.

One of the things I have encountered in a corporate prayer setting, specifically when a group of people are praying for someone, is that in their zeal, people will often pray over each other, using their outside voice. This is confusing and overwhelming for those being prayed for, and they may miss something the Lord wants them to hear because they are trying to listen to everyone at once. Let one start out, then the others wait their turn. People who are praying need to be secure enough that if someone else has prayed what the Lord has laid on your heart, you don't need to repeat the same thing. Be content with knowing that you were praying in the unity of the Holy Spirit.

Other Types of Prayer

There are many other types of prayer, but the effectiveness they hold starts with the depths of your relationship with the Father, through Jesus Christ. The power and authority that God allows to flow through you is dependent upon how much you allow the Holy Spirit to teach and transform you… meaning you use it to accomplish God's purposes and His glory, not yours.

One tactic the enemy uses against us in order to hinder our prayer life is accusation. He tries to plant a seed of doubt through accusation, and instead of us taking it captive, we believe it and allow it to take root. Then we quit praying, because we've allowed guilt or shame to re-establish the veil to separate us from Father God. Jesus, through the work of the Cross, tore down the veil that separated us from Almighty God (Matthew 27:51). There is NOTHING that can put that separation back, except us, through believing lies.

The Prayer of Confession – This glorious prayer is not a one-time prayer. It's an every-time-we-mess-up prayer. The prayer of confession keeps our hearts right before God. The key to this one is confessing, repenting (not going to do it again), being given and receiving forgiveness, then celebrating the TRUTH that you have been forgiven, believing it, and moving forward. Because the next tactic of the flesh and enemy is the thought, "I really haven't been forgiven." When you allow that thought to take precedence over TRUTH, you are saying that Almighty God and the Blood of Jesus Christ are not enough (Psalm 51:2-3).

The Prayer of Commitment – The prayer of commitment is dedicating your life to God. I pray this prayer regularly. I do not pray this because I don't think it didn't take the first time, but because it serves as a reminder to me, and as a declaration that I am committed to following the Lord (1 Peter 5:7).

The Prayer of Listening – This is one of the most overlooked and difficult prayers to nurture in one's life. Some may call these times practicing the presence of God. It's difficult because we must wait upon the Lord, and not fill that time thinking about what else we could be accomplishing. I am now capable of sitting in a room and shutting everything else out to wait upon the Lord. It took practice to get to that place. It's much easier for me to be still and listen for Him in nature. Getting outside, away from my to-do list, computer, laundry and other daily grinds of life, allows me to focus on Him and breathe Him in.

The Prayer of Fellowship – This type of prayer may best be described as keeping God amid everyday life. You're folding laundry: "Hi, God, how are you doing today?" You're at work: "Holy Spirit, I have a presentation to do, would you guide me through it?" You're driving home: "Lord, that was fun." Or: "Lord, that was difficult, help me to work through it please." It's simply talking to God about your life. If you think God doesn't have time for that, you are mistaken. God loves and desires these moments with His children (1 Thessalonians 5:16-18).

The Prayer of Thanksgiving – A prayer of gratefulness. These prayers are from a heart that understands and acknowledges the goodness of God. You're cleaning the toilet: "Lord, thank you for indoor plumbing." Sounds funny, but how would you like to clean an outhouse? Regardless of how challenging your life may be, there is always, always something to thank the Lord for. It's in the perspective (1 Thessalonians 5:18).

The Prayer of Praise – Praise declares who God is. Praise proclaims what He has done. Praise affirms what God has promised to do. Praying praise will lift your spirit in ways you would never think possible. Praise is a celebration! The Psalms are filled with prayers of praise. I encourage you to start there, then allow the Holy Spirit to teach you your personal prayers of praise (Exodus 15:2).

The Prayer of Worship – The best way I can describe the difference between praise and worship is that worship is more subdued; it's humbling ourselves before Him. The prayer of worship takes many postures—bowing, kneeling, even lying prostrate on the ground. There is a reverence about the prayer of worship different from other types of prayer. His glory manifests in a different way, and it quickens something inside us that recognizes the majesty and holiness of the Everlasting Father. When His glory manifests, our response may be tears of joy, tears of sorrow, silence, or even an inability to move. Regardless of the response, we always come away from these sacred moments forever changed. We know that we know the God we worship is the great I AM (Psalm 95:6).

The Prayer of Scripture – Praying Scripture calls forth the Lord to back His Word with His power and authority. 2 Peter 3:9 tells us that God is not willing that any should perish. That tells us we have His power and authority to pray for lost loved ones. When someone feels like the Lord has left them, Hebrews 13:5 tells us Jesus Himself said He would never leave nor forsake us. Praying Scripture is powerful because you pray God's Will. You pray His Word back to Him. Just remember that in order to pray Scripture, you need to know Scripture.

The Prayer of Agreement – This prayer is when one or more are praying together. As in corporate prayer, the prayer of agreement is to focus on what God wants to accomplish, and there needs to be unity. The prayer of agreement is powerful—more powerful than we realize. According to Matthew 18:19-20, when we agree here on earth, and ask, then it will be done for them by the Father who is in heaven. And, importantly, Jesus is in the midst of our prayer. The agreement comes in because we desire God's Will to be done, not ours.

The Prayer of Intercession – Intercession is such an incredible privilege God invites us to be a part of. Intercession is the Holy Spirit leading us to pray for God's Will for the needs of a person, place or cause. It's the opportunity for destinies and nations to be changed. The Holy Spirit will prompt us about something, and too often we brush these promptings off, not realizing that God wants to utilize us to bring heaven to earth. These promptings might come when we see something on the news and our heart either becomes angry or broken. I say angry because our spirit, in tune with the Holy Spirit, knows that it's not God's Will for that to be happening. Remember, anger—when under control—is not a sin. Anger can alert us to something that isn't right. I get angry about human trafficking, so it's often a topic of prayer. Intercession comes in when we see something not in alignment with God's Word, and we intervene on their behalf and petition God to bring forth His Will.

You want to see heaven come to earth? Cultivate an intercessor's passion to bring heaven forth. God will use you mightily for His Kingdom.

The Prayers of Request or Supplication – These prayers are similar to intercession, but normally more personal. These prayers are about seeing a need and praying over it. If you have a financial need, there is nothing selfish about praying over it. God will respond in your best interest. He may bring unexpected provision supernaturally or provide a way to earn extra money. It will most likely also include you having to do some practical work like a budget, preparing for a different type job, etc.

The Prayer of the Prophetic – These equipping, encouraging and empowering prayers are hearing a Word from the Lord for someone and praying it over them. It's calling out the greatness the Lord has placed inside them and calling it forth. There is nothing to fear from operating in prophetic prayers, but you must be on guard to only pray what the Lord prompts you to pray. These prayers have done too much damage in people's lives because of a lack of understanding of the prophetic and getting personal opinions mixed into the prayers.

God allows me to pray in the prophetic for people. But I've learned to be on high alert when I'm praying for people I know. It is easy to get your personal thoughts and opinion in the prayer based on the personal knowledge you have of the person or situation. Don't avoid praying for those you know; just be aware and ask the Holy Spirit to let you speak only what God wants to be spoken.

The Prayer of Praying in Tongues – There is so much division and controversy around this beautiful gift of praying in tongues. I encourage you to study praying in tongues directly from the Word of God and determine for yourself. Scripture is quite instructive on this type of prayer and how to operate in it, privately and in a corporate setting. Anything else is operating out of order and in the flesh. Praying in tongues is praying in an unknown language, and it's most powerfully used when we do not know what to pray. Praying in tongues prays the perfect Will of God into a situation because it's your spirit to the Holy Spirit. Our minds are removed from the process. I will say, though, that when I pray in tongues, I will often get a word in my mind and I know it's what I need to pray forth in my native language. Praying in tongues and in the understanding are both powerful (Romans 8:26-27, 1 Corinthians 14:14-15).

The Prayer of Warfare – These prayers confront the enemy and his kingdom, utilizing the weapons God has given us to do battle. Ephesians 6 outlines those weapons. Every follower of Christ should mature to the place where they know they operate in the authority of Almighty God and the enemy does not scare them. This is not to be ignorant, to think the enemy can't be a formidable foe. It is being secure in your relationship with the Lord and operating in His power and authority.

Acts 19:11-20 tells the story of seven sons of Sceva who tried to do warfare based on Paul's relationship with Jesus Christ instead of their own. It didn't work out too well for them. Operating in the prayers of warfare is vital to a follower of Christ, but again, the power and authority God delegates to you is dependent upon your relationship with Him.

The Prayers of Praying for One's Enemies – I saved this one for last, because it can be one of the most challenging. It is also the most Christ-like and requires a level of revelation that God loves everyone, even those who have hurt or wronged us. Yes, it might take a while to get to the place where we can sincerely pray for our 'enemies,' but we have a responsibility to do so. Jesus teaches us in Matthew 5:44-48 to love our enemies, to bless those who curse us and do good to those who hate us. He instructs us to *"...pray for those who spitefully use you and persecute you..."* As a follower of Christ, we are to pray, to intercede, on behalf of those who have harmed us. They, whether you agree or not, deserve to experience the grace and mercy of God. Remember, if it were not for the grace of God, we would be in a much different place from where we are now.

The Word of God instructs us to pray unceasingly. We think unceasing prayer is an impossible task, but with God, all things are possible.

When we sin, pray.

When we lose sight of who we belong to, pray.

When we feel empty, pray.

When we feel alone, pray.

When we are grateful, pray.

When we are joyous, pray.

When we need more, pray.

When we need power, pray.

When we need encouragement, pray.

When we need mountains to move, pray.

When we need lives to change, pray.

When we have a need, pray.

When greatness needs to be called out, pray.

When we don't know what to pray, pray.

When we are sick and tired of the enemy destroying lives, pray.

When we desire to have the heart of Christ, pray.

> *"Be anxious for nothing, but in everything by prayer and supplication, with thanksgiving, let your requests be made known to God; and the peace of God, which surpasses all understanding, will guard your hearts and minds through Christ Jesus."* (Philippians 4:6-7)

Prayer is not optional in the life of a follower of Christ. Prayer needs to become a priority in your life, and a part of everything you do. When you are intentional about prayer, talking to the Father, it becomes as natural as breathing. Don't miss out on the glorious gift of prayer.

CHAPTER 12

Pressing Toward the Goal

"I press toward the goal for the prize of the upward call of God in Christ Jesus." (Philippians 3:14)

Paul, who penned these words, was used by the Lord to take the Good News of Jesus Christ to Jews, Gentiles (anyone who wasn't Jewish), Romans, Greeks, slaves and free persons. He was a Pharisee, which was the elite of the elite in Jewish religion. He also participated in the imprisonment, torturing and killing of Christians. Yet, despite his past, the Lord used him to accomplish great and mighty things for the Kingdom of God.

One of the keys I propose that kept him pursuing his purpose is found in the verses before verse 14:

> *"Not that I have already attained, or am already perfected; but I press on, that I may lay hold of that for which Christ Jesus has also laid hold of me. Brethren, I do not count myself to have apprehended; but one thing I do, forgetting those things which are behind and reaching forward to those things which are ahead..."* (Philippians 3:12-13)

Paul knew he hadn't attained all he needed to accomplish. He knew he wasn't perfect. But he had a determination to move forward. He knew he didn't have all the answers, but he was confident in the One who does.

Perhaps the most liberating thing was that Paul grabbed hold of the truth that he could not change his past. He could only put his past in the past, forgetting those things, and reaching forward to the things the Lord had for him. I will say that we do need to be healed of our past, so it no longer holds us in bondage or distorts our perspective.

But too many people live in the past. They blame the past for their problems, difficult personality traits, unhealthy behaviors, poor choices and current circumstances.

You cannot change your past, but you can change how you see it. Everything in your past that was meant for harm, God can turn and use for good.

Paul was made free through the truth of Jesus Christ. You have been made free through the Truth of Jesus Christ. It is time to keep your eye on Jesus and press toward the upward call of God found in Him.
You carry the Kingdom of God with you. You carry Jesus Christ within you. The Holy Spirit resides within you. Everywhere your sole treads, the Lord your God is with you.

You have been given everything needed to be healed from hurts, set free from lies, and restored from lost time. God has provided everything required for you to do the work and be made free.

The Lord gave a promise to Jeremiah, and it is just as applicable to every child of God: *"For I know the thoughts that I think toward you, says the Lord, thoughts of peace and not of evil, to give you a future and a hope."*

God has given you a future and a hope. It's up to you to pursue and live it out, or not.

God has fearfully and wonderfully made you. He has given you good and perfect gifts. You have everything at your disposal to be equipped and fulfill the plans and purposes God has for you. He will prosper the work of your hands when the work is for His glory.

Keep pressing forward.

The command is the same for all followers of Jesus Christ:

> *"And Jesus came and spoke to them, saying, 'All authority has been given to Me in heaven and on earth. Go therefore and make disciples of all the nations, baptizing them in the name of the Father and of the Son and of the Holy Spirit, teaching*

them to observe all things that I have commanded you; and lo, I am with you always, even to the end of the age.'" (Matthew 28:18-20)

This command is a part of our calling, our purpose. It is part of what defines us as His. The degree to which it is fulfilled is dependent upon the position God has placed us in. But making disciples is possible everywhere.

Fathers and Mothers disciple their children.

CEOs disciple their employees.

Employees can disciple other employees.

Small group leaders facilitate teaching to equip the saints.
Children's and Youth ministries disciple children.

I plant a seed with a cashier at the checkout stand. Another comes along and waters. Then the Lord has another harvest the fruit of all who labored.

One invites someone to church. Another welcomes them through the doors. Another meets with them for coffee. Another prays for them. Another teaches them.

These are only a few examples of making disciples and how you can participate in the process of discipling others, so they are made free in Christ Jesus. It's about being part of the world-wide Body of Christ. There is one God, one Savior, one Spirit and one Body.

There is a parable about an old man, a little boy and thousands of starfish. It goes like this:

One day, an old man was walking along a beach that was littered with thousands of starfish that had been washed ashore by the high tide. As he walked, he came upon a young boy who was eagerly throwing the starfish back into the ocean, one by one.

Puzzled, the man looked at the boy and asked what he was doing. Without looking up from his task, the boy simply replied, "I'm saving these starfish, Sir."

The old man chuckled aloud. "Son, there are thousands of starfish and only one of you. What difference can you make?"

The boy picked up a starfish, gently tossed it into the water and turning to the man, said, "I made a difference to that one!" (www.starfishproject. com)

Can you imagine how many more starfish would have been set free if the older man had joined the young man in the task, rather than laughing and trying to discourage the boy by the size of the task?

You may be called to disciple ten, hundreds, even thousands. You may be called to disciple one, and it is just as important as the one who is called to disciple more. To that one person, you will make all the difference.

You are a part of changing a person's destiny, and there is no greater honor than that.

In your pursuit to become all you are in Christ Jesus, remember that part of your purpose is to help others become all they are in Him as well. Love God. Love others.

You have been MADE FREE. Embrace a life lived in freedom…

> *"Heavenly Father, I thank You for wanting me to be made free by Your love and Word. I know You love me and work all things to my good and Your glory. Fill me with Your Holy Spirit, so I am taught Your Truths and abide in Your Son, Jesus Christ. I know this is a lifetime journey; help me to keep pursuing You all the days of my life. Renew my mind and transform my life. Help me to love you and to love others. In Jesus' Name I pray. Amen."*

PART 3

Final Encouragement

"The thief does not come EXCEPT to steal, and to kill, and to destroy. I have come that they may have life, AND THAT THEY MAY HAVE IT MORE ABUNDANTLY." (John 10:10, emphasis added)

The enemy is real, and he will try everything he can to steal your identity and blessings. He is focused on killing your dreams and purpose. If given the opportunity, he will destroy everything about you and those you love. I'm not being a little intense—we have a real enemy. And he is still prowling around like a lion seeking whom he may devour.

Jesus Christ defeated the enemy with the work at the Cross. He came so that not only you could have life, but that you would have it more abundantly. THE MESSAGE versions says it like this: *"I came so they can have real and eternal life, more and better life than they EVER DREAMED OF."*

That is quite a promise... to have life more and better than we could ever dreamed of!

God has given us access to everything we need to live free and abundantly. Through Christ Jesus, and the gift of the Holy Spirit, we can be made free and live free all the days of our lives.

Yes, we will encounter challenging and difficult times. There will be times of disappointment, pain, and grief. And yes, there will be times when evil will touch our lives. But... God. Jesus said we would have trouble in this world, and would have trouble because of our belief in Him. He also tells us, *"Be of good cheer because I have overcome the world."*

Through every joy and heartache, Jesus is with us. Through every mistake and wrong choice, Jesus is there. Through every victory and defeat, Jesus is in the fight with us. For every success and every failure, Jesus, with a great crowd of witnesses, is cheering us on.

Embrace a Life Lived in Freedom!

With Hope,
Your sister in Christ,
Tracy

ACKNOWLEDGMENTS

My life is a result of the graciousness and the faithfulness of the God I serve. He has never given up on me, even when I gave up on Him and myself. My life is a testimony to the love of God and the Truth of His promise to bring beauty from ashes. Father God, thank You for all You are. To my mom Paula and my mom Eva, thank you for always believing in me. To my husband, children and grandchildren, I am rich because of you. My wonderfully steadfast friends who stand by me, call, text, or email at just the right moment, hold me accountable and keep encouraging me to finish this race well, I love you beyond words. To the Prayer Partners and Missions Team at Freedom Church, Carrollton, Texas, it's a joy to advance the Kingdom of God with you. To the Freedom Church Family, it's an honor to do life with you. I am truly blessed beyond measure!

Keep being Made Free for the glory of God!

ABOUT THE AUTHOR

Tracy L. Edwards was born and raised in south Texas. She grew up in the country raising show animals and riding horses at rodeos. She married her husband Steve in 1995 and they have three children and two grandchildren. She enjoys reading, writing, trying to grow plants, going on adventures with her family, and working with her husband on their land. Her passion is to see people experience the love of God and fulfill the purpose they were born for. Her heart is to see people live in the hope, peace and joy that is available through the truth found in a personal relationship with Jesus Christ.

She loves to speak, teach and equip others to embrace a life lived with purpose and passion.

You can contact her at:

Email: up-word@outlook.com

Website: Up-WordBound.com